The Relevance of Preaching

The Relevance of Preaching

The Basics of Homiletics and
Preaching for Preachers

Perumalla Surya Prakash

Christian World Imprints

First Published in 2025 by

Christian World Imprints
Christian Publishing & Books from India
A-71 Group, Wazirpur Industrial Area
Delhi-110052
cwidelhi2017@gmail.com
www.ChristianWorldImprints.com
Phone: +91 11 41526079

ISBN: 978-93-6065-069-8

Book Cover: Pulpit in Medak Cathedral of the Church of South India

Design: Amritha Bosi

Cover page image of the pulpit in Medak Cathedral used by permission.

Printed in India.

Dedication of the Book on Preaching:

The book is dedicated to the loving memory
of my Professors on Preaching, namely
Dr. John E. Skoglund of United States and
Dr. Traugott Staehlin and
Dr. Gerhard Ruhback of Germany.
With ever grateful thanks,
Author

Contents

Acknowledgements

I gratefully acknowledge my deep sense of gratitude to my senior presbyters in the Diocese of Medak, Bishops in Medak, and homiletic professors at United Theological College Bengaluru and Kirchliche Hochschule Bethel Bielefeld Germany, who influenced me in effective preaching.

I am equally thankful to my mentors in Preaching, namely the Rev. Dr. A. B. Masilamany and Bishop Peddi Victor Prema Sagar, Bishop Badda Peter Sugandhar and Rev. Dr. Dass Babu in their impact on my ministry of preaching.

My thanks to the librarians of the above mentioned libraries, Mrs. E. Adiappa, Mrs.Rita Gurupadam, Mr. Buchmann and Mrs. Ruth Bimler.

I remember my students at UTC, Bengaluru to whom the principles and methods presented here in preaching were demonstrated.

Above all, I am ever thankful to my dear family, my wife Mrs. Hitha Vachini Vindhya Rani, daughters Amritha Bosi and Sarah Prathibha for their unstinched support.

Equally thankful to my grand children, Nathan, Norah and Navitha for their love. They have assisted their mother in designing the cover page.

May God bless them all.

My thanks to Christian World Imprints for publishing and printing the book.

Preface

This book on preaching reflects on the basics of Christian preaching in Indian context. In the modern age of technological advancement, scientific explorations and social media, the book seeks to provide insights into the age-old art of preaching and its relevance. There are people who take preaching for granted in their ministry in the church. There are also others who take the ministry of preaching seriously. It is to such preachers; this book will be a great help. It is simple but deals with profound subjects.

– Author

Foreword-I

While deeming it a privilege to be asked by the author to write a *Forward* for this book, I also consider it to be a pleasant task to pen a few lines to my companion and partner in the ecumenical movement in India and particularly in the Telugu Region. While he was the Bishop of CSI Diocese in Karimnagar during 2007 to 2014, Prof. Dr. P. Surya Prakash also served as the General Secretary of Andhra Pradesh Federation of Churches (APFC), now renamed as the Federation of Telugu Churches (FTC), which is the apex body and fellowship of Bishops and Heads of major Churches in the Telugu States. Having heard his sermons and inspired and enlightened by them, several times I extended invitations to him to address ecumenical gatherings. However, what surprises one is the deep commitment he has for the ministry of preaching, hard work that he puts in to prepare them by way of intense study and prayerful reflection. In the *Introduction* to this book, he shares with the reader, the serious efforts he made to become a good preacher and a professor of Homiletics. His interest, motivation, enthusiasm and endeavour in this subject itself is very moving and inspiring. This book in your hand, therefore, is a result of his experience and engagement, study and research, and teaching and preaching. It is the reason why he is able to present in this volume simple but profound manner both the theory / theology and praxis / practice of Christian preaching.

Every Christian, as a disciple of the Lord Jesus Christ, is mandated to continue His mission of preaching the Gospel of the Kingdom of God, while the pastors have accepted to commit themselves full time for this ministry. To all of them, this book, as its title says, attempts to be bring out the *relevance* of preaching. The relevance of preaching very much depends on the "Context." The text of one's preaching is made relevant only when it is relevant to the present context of the listeners. A dialogue needs to take place between the past context of the text being preached and the present context of the listeners. Or else, the preaching would turn out to be sowing on the rocky ground, they would not get rooted (cfr. Mt 13.21). A context entails social status, economic stratification, political position, cultural situation, religious background and environmental condition. Hence, we need to know them, before preaching to a group of people. For an effective preaching in the multi-cultural and multi-religious context of India, we need to also keep in mind, the psychological make up, cultural mind set, world view, outlook, social fabric and intertwining relationships of the listeners.

To cite the example of Apostle Paul, who laid strong foundations for preaching the Gospel, he first preached to the Jews, and then to the Greeks and so called Gentiles. He had two sets of sermons, so to say, one to the Jews and another to the others. To the Jews, he recalls their election, convent, exodus, Davidic heritage and the promise of messiah focussing on the "particular salvation history" found in the Bible (cfr. Acts 13.14-52). To the Greeks and others who belong to different religions and cultures, basing himself on the "universal salvation history", Paul's sermons stress that God is the creator of whole creation and humanity including all the peoples and nations and has revealed Himself to all (cf. Acts 17:16-34). His preaching was contextual, historical, Biblical and relevant to the people of a particular place and time, thus, setting an example for all the preachers.

In the current socio-political scenario of India, we are faced with increasing attacks on the preachers, and mounting obstacles for the proclamation of the Gospel. Every day, not less than two incidents of violence are recorded on the Christians and pastors in India, and even conducting prayers is becoming difficult in some places. This socio-political context call for reviewing and re-visioning of our mission of preaching and establishing the Kingdom of God in India. Helpful in this urgent task is the joint document that is widely accepted by most of the Churches: *Christian Witness in a Multi-Religious World: Recommendations for Conduct.* It urges all the Christians to preach and evangelise, however, "it is necessary to do so according to gospel principles, with full respect and love for all human beings." This ecumenical document was finalised after a period of 5 years reflection in 2011, to respond to the tensions between people and communities of different religious convictions by the Pontifical Council for Interreligious Dialogue (RCC-PCID) of the Roman Catholic Church, World Council of Churches' Programme on Interreligious Dialogue and Co-operation (WCC-IRDC), and the World Evangelical Alliance (WEA). Its purpose is to serve as a set of recommendations for conduct on Christian witness around the world and to address practical issues associated with Christian witness in a multi-religious world. One of its several recommendations is regarding preaching in a multi-religious context: "Christians are to speak sincerely and respectfully; they are to listen in order to learn about and understand others' beliefs and practices, and are encouraged to acknowledge and appreciate what is true and good in them. Any comment or critical approach should be made in a spirit of mutual respect, making sure not to bear false witness concerning other religions." Hence, while preaching in the Indian context, it is important to be sensitive to the religious sentiments of the listeners so as not to hurt them.

Let me conclude with a word of appreciation and gratitude to the authour Bishop Emeritus Surya Prakash, who even after his retirement keeps making significant contribution as an academic, ecumenical activist and administrator to the Church taking into consideration not only the mainline Churches but the small, independent, and indigenous Churches in India as well. Not only the present volume, he has also authored several articles that were published in famous journals. He is a sought after as a preacher and worship leader, and regularly invited to address and present papers in the national symposiums and ecumenical seminars. May God bless him with good health to continue his valuable contribution and fruitful ministry for many more years to come, and may his tribe increase!

Rev. Fr Dr Anthoniraj Thumma
National Secretary of Office for Dialogue and Desk for Ecumenism of the Catholic Bishops' Conference of India (CBCI) & Coordinator of National Ecumenical Bishops' Fellowship
New Delhi, May 19, 2025

Foreword-II

In every generation, the Church stands at a crossroads, challenged to speak with clarity, conviction, and compassion to a world in flux. Amid cultural upheavals, technological revolutions, and shifting moral landscapes, one question remains vital: Is preaching still relevant?

This book, Relevance of Preaching, addresses that question with theological depth, historical awareness, and pastoral insight. Rooted in a high view of Scripture and an unwavering commitment to the gospel, the author calls preachers back to the heart of their calling—proclaiming the Word of God with relevance, faithfulness, and urgency.

The chapters explore not only the biblical and theological foundations of preaching but also its practical outworking in a postmodern context. From the centrality of Christ in every message to the preacher's personal holiness, the book challenges both new and seasoned ministers to examine their motives, sharpen their methods, and deepen their spiritual lives.

What makes this work particularly compelling is its insistence that preaching is not merely a religious speech or a motivational talk, but a divine appointment—where heaven meets earth through the foolishness of the spoken word. In a time when pulpits are often tempted to trade conviction for popularity, Relevance of Preaching is a clarion call to return to bold, biblical, Spirit-empowered proclamation.

Rt. Rev. Dr. Surya Prakash brings to this work not only years of academic study and ecclesiastical leadership but also the heart of a pastor and the soul of a preacher. As a bishop, theologian, and teacher of preachers across denominational lines, his passion for faithful proclamation shines through every page. This book is the fruit of a life deeply rooted in the Word and devoted to the ministry of preaching.

Whether you are a pastor, seminary student, or someone yearning for truth, this book will reignite your passion for preaching and remind you of its enduring power to transform lives. May it inspire a new generation to stand up, speak out, and preach the Word—faithfully, boldly, and relevantly.

Dr. Packiam T. Samuel
Director-HMI, Hyderabad

Foreword-III

The word of God has the power to transform our heart, mind and soul. However, in this fast-paced, digitally driven and multi-sensorial world where people would like to hear, see and touch to experience the power of anything that can impact their lives, the question of relevance of the word especially the spoken word is much important today than ever before. Jesus our master and saviour commanded his disciples to preach, teach, heal and make disciples. Even after His resurrection, Jesus commissioned his disciples to go into the world lead people from darkness into marvellous light, from death into everlasting life. So, preaching has served as a conduit for truth, transformation, hope and comfort. Yet in a world inundated with competing voices, contradictory statements, confounding dogmas this book comes timely giving direction to every preacher to understand the nuances of the art of preaching and making it relevant.

Bishop Surya Prakash Perumalla by combining his passion for preaching and teaching homiletics at UTC for 10 years makes a resounding affirmation of the role of the Word of God in the life of the Church and individuals by explaining what is Christian preaching, where and how to preach, how the word of God was preached in the New Testament times and how is it done in 21st Century, and most importantly how word of God ought to be shared in a multi-religious context. It is not enough to have passion for preaching but every preacher must know these essentials so that it does not repel but attract people towards the light and life

Jesus offers; it doesn't become a tool to hurt the listeners but heal them. Sermon preparation plans and the importance of theology in interpreting the word of God to read the signs of our times and prepare the church to face the realities is a unique contribution. Finally, insights for conducting Bible Studies makes this book a must read. His work thoroughly explores how preachers today can speak into their communities with clarity, conviction and compassion. It reminds us that preaching, when taken seriously with all the tools provided in this book can not only become relevant but transformative.

Sermons be it thematic or textual, narrative or expository must always be contextual. They connect with the sitz-im- leben of the text as well as the present-day context thus it becomes relevant at all times. Bishop Surya Prakash rightly says that the 'Preaching in the 21st century will start by reading the gospel from the places of hurt and injustice that is so much prevalent in the society. From there, we start to make sense of the Bible and our own contexts. A sermon is to relate the text to the context.' Primary task of the preaching, as he mentions is 'not for self-projection, image building or money making' but to reveal the purposes of God towards his creation, affirm the dignity and equality of all, establish peace and harmony, inspire a just and egalitarian society, prepare the believers for the coming of Christ and certainly to condemn the wrong.

This book delineating the importance of preaching within the church and outside helps the readers to understand that the sermons have the ability to connect the eternal and the contemporary; they have the ability to call for 'reflection-action-change' that can bring about reformation. I wish and pray that the preachers would gain needed insights to make their preachings meaningful, relevant and transformative.

Finally, I express my sincere thanks to Bishop Surya Prakash Perumalla, who taught me Homiletics during my Batchelor of Divinity at UTC, for asking me to write the foreword for this book. His teachings have enabled me to bring out Sermon Outlines (*Kristu Jignasa*) for the 3-year lectionary cycle during my tenure as the Director of the Department of Pastoral Concerns, CSI Synod. Writing this foreword was the most humbling and at the same time an enriching experience.

Rev. Dr. K. James Cecil Victor
B.Sc., B.D., M.Th., D.Min
Presbyter, Medak Diocese

Foreword-IV

In an age dominated by digital engagement, instant communication, and ideological fragmentation, the timeless art of preaching remains a crucial vehicle for spiritual formation, theological reflection, and social transformation. The Relevance of Preaching by Bishop Emeritus P. Surya Prakash is both a timely and timeless contribution that reclaims the centrality of the pulpit within the life of the Church and society.

Rooted deeply in scripture, enriched by academic insight, and shaped through decades of pastoral and teaching ministry, this work offers a profound synthesis of homiletical tradition, contextual theology, and practical wisdom. Bishop Prakash brings to the table not only theological acumen but also the pastoral heart of one who has walked closely with congregations, clergy, students, and diverse communities across continents.

This book does more than define preaching — it forms preachers. From outlining the biblical mandate and spiritual discipline of sermon preparation, to examining preaching in the 21st century and in multi-religious contexts, it equips both emerging and experienced ministers with tools to navigate complex realities with courage, clarity, and compassion.

For theological educators, seminarians, pastors, and all those who seek to proclaim the Word with authenticity and relevance, this text serves as a foundational resource. It challenges the complacent, encourages the discouraged, and inspires a new generation to preach with conviction, grace, and integrity.

May this work strengthen the ministry of preaching and serve as a reminder that in every age and circumstance, the faithful proclamation of the gospel remains indispensable to the mission of the Church.

Rev. Dr. U. Daniel
Bsc, BD, MTh, D.Min
Presbyter In Charge
CSI Church of St John the Baptist
Secunderabad, TS. India

Book Commendation-I

The Relevance of Preaching: The Basics of Homiletics and Preaching for Preachers is a comprehensive and relevant book for all who are active in the ministry of the Church. It is a book that provides not only the basics of preaching but also a detailed study of the praxis of preaching. From guiding the readers on Exegesis to Sermon preparations, Bible Study to understanding the Theology and Authority of Preaching, this book is a wonderful tool for theological students, lay persons and pastors. Written by Bishop Perumalla Surya Prakash whose 40+ year ministry in the Church as a prolific preacher, New Testament scholar, eminent theologian, bishop and pastor, this book is a deep reflection of his commitment to the art of preaching. It is a timely and poignant book that is highly recommended to all who want to engage and broaden their understanding of preaching in the Church.

Amritha Bosi, Hannover, Germany
May 2025

Book Commendation-II

The Relevance of Preaching is a timely and insightful guide that reaffirms the enduring significance of preaching in a rapidly evolving world. With clarity and depth, Bishop Surya Prakash explores the biblical foundation, historical development, and contemporary challenges of Christian preaching, especially in the Indian context. At its core, the book emphasizes that preaching remains a vital act of faith formation, spiritual guidance, and communal transformation — provided it is rooted in discipline, Scripture, and dependence on the Holy Spirit. Drawing from decades of pastoral experience, global academic exposure, and a deep personal passion, Bishop Surya Prakash equips both new and seasoned preachers with practical tools, theological insight, and a renewed sense of calling. This book is not just a manual, but a heartfelt invitation to engage preaching as a dynamic and Spirit-led ministry that continues to bear fruit where the Word finds good soil.

Dr. Sarah Perumalla, Berlin, Germany
May 2025

Introduction

Is preaching still relevant today? This is a question that is asked many times these days.

There is so much preaching going on in the world and in India. There is no Sunday without a sermon. In India there is no prayer meeting without a sermon. I ask myself this question of relevance because of the following reasons.

Almost nobody asks the preacher a question. There are no sermon discussion groups. We don't see any reaction and no response. Has it simply become a liturgical element? Has it simply become a worship event? Or is it a professional requirement of pastors and others who engage in preaching? As I ponder over these questions, the parable of the Sower comes to my mind. Jesus tells a wonderful parable and explains its meaning. The Sower goes and sows. And the seeds fall on four different places in the field. Some on the roadside, others under the thorny bushes, some others on the rocky soil. But some fall on the good soil. Jesus does not describe the field but emphasizes on the yield. It looks as though the field is not prepared well. But Jesus interest is in the result.

So also, in our churches and congregations, some seeds always fall on good soil. The spirit of God works in them. We do not give up. It can become relevant if we follow certain discipline and depend on the spirit of God. Let us explore them.

Preaching has been my passion from childhood. I always wanted to be a preacher. While for bachelor's in divinity (B.D.)

at the United Theological College Bengaluru (UTC), we had a well experienced visiting professor of preaching, namely Dr. John Skoglund. He impressed me most and I chose for writing my thesis on the relationship between preaching and counselling. He was my guide too. One day I hope to publish it.

I kept my interest in preaching and throughout my pastoral ministry it was always my passion. I would write down my sermons. During my college days, I have copied about 100 sermons of Billy Graham by hand from Decision Magazine in five notebooks (Unfortunately, they are lost in the course of time). I would go into bushes and practice preaching in my village during my vacation time.

Later, when I wanted to do my doctorate in theology, encouraged by UTC, I undertook research into Homiletics (the art of preaching) in a German University and chose, the preaching of Sadhu Sundar Singh as my specialisation. The book has been published and republished.

Having taught homiletics at UTC for 10 years and trained students to become teachers of preaching while doing their master's in theology, I have developed more experience and have come to know many professors and authors on preaching. My interaction with professors of homiletics at Princeton Theological Seminary, Princeton USA (PTS) during my short period of Speech Communication training in 1993, I have met some eminent teachers of preaching. The collection of books in the PTS library impressed me beyond my imagination. Being a member of the Academy of Homileticians in Germany in 1980s, I was simply overwhelmed by the scholars and teachers of preaching and their scholarship.

While teaching in different continents and doing ministry among different churches ecumenically during my sabbatical at San Francisco Theological Seminary, San Francisco in 1997 and in Church College Bethel Bielefeld, Mission Seminar in Hermannsburg, Germany, the passion for preaching has simply become a way of life for me. During my tenure as Diocesan

Bishop in Karimnagar of the Church of South India from 2007 to 2014, it was a privilege to preach on every Sunday at a different church in the diocese. I have always followed the lectionary of the church. I would like to share it in this basic book on preaching to all interested and committed preachers. There are plenty of books on preaching available particularly in the West, but not in our country.

Therefore, this is a sincere attempt to help pastors and preachers based on my years of experience and exposure ecumenically and internationally.

The book does not try to provide all answers but leaves the interested pastors and preachers to think creatively and do their best in the light of insights provided.

It is a kind of preparatory workbook for learners and young preachers.

The relevance of preaching depends on many factors. We shall explore some of them.

Chapter 1

What is Christian Preaching?

Preaching is a regular activity of the church all over the world particularly on Sundays at worship services.

a. Preaching is a Biblical Imperative

2 Timothy 4.2, preach the Gospel.

St. Mathew 28.18-20, preaching, teaching, and making disciples: the mandate given to the disciples. This is commonly known as the great commission.

1 Timothy 5.17, labour in teaching and preaching.

Acts 6.2, not to neglect the word of God.

Mark 3.14, to be sent out to preach.

Micah 2.11, prophet is a preacher for his people.

St. Paul: Woe unto me if I do not preach the gospel. I Corinthians 9.16.

Christian Preaching is by the church, for the church and society.

Preaching is basically of two types:

1. **Preaching within the Church**
    - Lectionary preaching. Planned Preaching according to the seasons of the church year. Advent, Christmas, Epiphany, Lent, Easter, Ascension, Pentecost, Trinity.
    - Free Preaching

Free churches and particularly the Baptists, the Pentecostals, and others.

It is the free selection of biblical passages and themes.

2. **Preaching Outside the Church**
    - It consists of revival meetings, or crusades or prayer festivals.

b. Understanding Preaching

Greek word "Homileia", meaning conversation, discussion, In English – Homily.

The art of preaching is called Homiletics, the science of preparation and delivery of sermons.

The Roman Catholics often use, homily.

In the NT, the word "Kerussein" in Greek is used, meaning proclamation publicly or public preaching.

Latin word "Sermo", means persuasive speech.

The Protestants normally use, sermon, coming from Sermo.

The Pentecostal, charismatic groups and evangelicals use, "message", "God's word".

c. Popular Definitions of Preaching

Philips Brooks, "preaching is communication of truth through the personality of the preacher." It is the most popular definition.

Truth here means the gospel and personality means the whole being of the preacher.

Message and medium are equally important.

W. E. Sangster, "preaching is, was and ever will be Gods chief way of communicating his will to the world."

Thomas Long, main elements of preaching:

a. Preacher – communicator

b. Message – sermon calling for action.

c. Congregation – hearers

d. Role of the Holy Spirit – presence of Christ

Preaching is the lifeline of the church and its mission.

d. Qualities of Preacher

a. Knowledge of God – the prophets speak in the name of God.

Thus says the Lord – "Co Aamar Jahweh" in Hebrew.

Consistent study of the Bible is a pre-requisite.

b. Fear of God – awe in the presence of God.

c. Love of God – if you love one another, you keep my commandment.

d. Passion for God and compassion for people.

e. Interpretation of the Word/Text

a. Allegorical – comparing the past and the present.

b. Ethical/Moral – application to the hearers.

c. Contextual – text to context, then and now.

d. Literal – as it is, taking the face value.

f. Preparation of the Sermon

a. Personal encounter with the living God.

b. Experiencing God's grace in Christ.

c. Theological education and systematic study.

d. Diligent and hard work of reflection, meditation, and prayer.

g. Classification of the Sermon

a. the Biblical
b. the Ethical
c. the Devotional
d. the Doctrinal
e. the Social
f. the Evangelical

h. Types of Preaching

i. Lectionary based or prescribed.
ii. Preacher's choice of the text.

i. Methods of Preaching

a. the Textual
b. the Topical
c. the Expository
d. the Narrative

j. Components of a Sermon

a. the Introduction
b. the Body
c. the Illustration
d. the Application
e. the Conclusion

k. Communication – Delivery of a Sermon

a. the Voice modulation
b. the Language
c. the Gestures
d. the Eye Contact
e. the Appearance

l. Contemporary Streams of Preaching

a. Preaching in the Church – church preaching in the context of worship.

b. Revival Preaching – preaching in the context of revival meetings.

c. TV Preaching – preaching in and through television.

d. Radio broadcasts.

m. Purpose of Preaching

a. Edification of the believers

b. Growing in Faith of the listeners

c. Deeper Understanding of the Scriptures by the church

d. Christian Living and Witnessing in the world

e. And Christian Mission in different Ways etc. in the society

f. Evangelisation, church planting, making new believers

g. Transformation of human beings

n. Preaching Outside of the Church

- Revival preachings
- Missionary preaching
- Evangelistic preaching
- Church Plantation etc.

Purpose: Evangelisation of the World

o. Preaching During Missionary Times

Three streams: Three types we could find.

- Exclusive claims: Absoluteness of Jesus was claimed and biblical texts like John 14.6 and Acts of the Apostles 4.12
- Inclusive claims: Acts of the Apostles 17, Paul, and Silas in Berea; Paul in Athens.
- Pluralistic understanding: 1 Corinthians 8 and other texts
- What could be the preaching now in a secular/multi-religious and multi-cultural societies? We will see later in the book.

Chapter 2

Do You Know – When, Where, What and How to Preach?

1. Who to Preach?

a. The one who is called by Jesus.
b. The one who is with Jesus.
c. The one who is trained.
d. The one who is sent into the world.
e. The who is called and sent by the church.

2. What to Preach?

a. The Gospel of Jesus Christ, the good news of salvation
b. The kingdom of God, family of God, a new community
c. The Cross, Death and Resurrection of Jesus, the means of salvation
d. Equipping the Saints for the Work of Ministry, of the word and sacraments.

No self-projection

No image building.

No money making.

No self-interests

but with humility and commitment

3. When to Preach?

Whenever an occasion demands.

St. Paul says, in season and out of season (2 Timothy 4.2).

4. Where to Preach?

At worship services

At evangelical/revival meetings

At house meetings

5. How to Preach?

With preparation by prayer, reflection and according to the context and the nature of the listeners

6. The Purpose of Preaching?

Equipping for the Work of the Ministry of the Church

'To equip the saints for the work of ministry, for building up the body of Christ'.

Ephesians 4:12 (NRSV)

Equipping is a great word used by St. Paul, in his letter to the Church in Ephesus.

Equipping: Training, Building, Forming, Growing, Developing,

Equipping the theological teachers and trainers for the ministry:

Understanding theology and theological education and theological institution.

Understanding theological teaching as a profession and also as a vocation in, of and by the church.

Understanding the nature of the church.

Understanding the ministry of the church.

Understanding the patterns and forms of ministry

A first-hand experience in the ministry is a must

Issues: The relationship between the college and church

The relationship of the teacher to the church

Equipping the pastors for the challenges of ministry:

Understanding the context of the ministry

Understanding the demands of ministry in the context

Recognising the challenges of the context

Issues: Theological education and training

Continuing education in the ministry

Ministers self-study or guided programme

Ministers meetings, weekly or monthly in the region or pastorate for study and prayers and reflection and discussion of issues

Equipping the congregations for a life of witnessing in the society:

Understanding the nature of the local congregation biblically, theologically and socially and culturally.

Analysing the congregation and its potentials and shortcomings

Equipping the Bishops and administrators for effective ministry:

Understanding the office of episcopacy

Understanding the biblical concept of leadership

Understanding modern demands of professionalism

Functions: Facilitating, coordinating, guiding, leading, shepherding, caring,

Issues: collegiality, transparency, accountability, the role of the family in the office of the leader

Equipping the teachers and trainers for the value-oriented education:

Equipping the medical doctors and para-medical staff for healing ministry:

Equipping the wardens and caretakers for effective child-care ministry:

Equipping the social workers for the ministry of justice:

a. Christ Academy of Preachers

Jesus sets an example of preaching.

Jesus's way of preparing the preachers: See St. Mark 3. 13-19

Professional Formation – to be effective preachers, good communicators.

Academic Formation – to be informed as preachers, well informed.

Personal Formation – to be qualified as preachers, ambassadors of Christ.

Chapter 3

What are the Names and Definitions of the Preacher among the Churches?

Moderator – one who moderates and presides over meetings.

Pastor – one who has the spiritual care of the congregation.

Priest – an official conductor of religious rituals

Clergy man/woman – ordained person

Church man/man – upholder of the established church

Minister – one who serves at the altar or table.

Abba – father

Padre – pastor or father

Presbyter – an elder

Curate – a subordinate clergy/deacon

Deacon – a servant, a servant of Jesus

Shepherd – one who takes care of the congregation.

Reverend – a person to be respected usually among the clergy.

Chaplain – a clergy attached to an institution.

Evangelist – one who evangelises, authorised to preach.

Revivalist – one who revives the congregation/Christians.

Missionary – one who is sent on a mission to preach.

Preacher – one who discourses publicly on religious matters.

Rector – a controller/ruler

Incumbent - the person in charge

Patriarch – one who rules.

Pope – Bishop in Rome

Canon – ecclesiastical authority

Vicar – an assistant to a pastor

Bishop – an overseer of the church

Archbishop – an overseer of the bishops

Cardinal – an overseer of the archbishops

Father – used mostly among the Catholics.

Primate – one who is first (archbishop or Bishop)

Theologian – one who is well versed in theology (science of God)

Pujari – the one who does puja (performance of rituals)

Pandit – the teacher/interpreter of the scriptures

Guru – religious teacher

Animate – one who conducts!

Teacher – one who teaches.

You see the preacher is a very important person in the society. Who else has so many titles and responsibilities with privileges and challenges?

Areas of reading for the preacher:

The Bible

Not just Bible alone but also human rights, scientific and technological advance, medical and psychological research, art, films, theatre, music and dance, fiction, television and mass communication, travel and anthropology, sociology and ethics, biblical and theological studies etc.

Preachers' health and recreation, read Pastoral Letters in the NT (Letters to Timothy and Titus).

Fitness is another important issue.

a. Physical fitness – exercise, diet and recreation (vacation). Appearance is important (Be handsome but modest). Establish suitable rhythm between work and relaxation. Get a proper amount of physical exercise. Maintain a suitable diet. Get a reasonable amount of sleep. Take frequent vacations. Learn to play every day.
b. Mental/Psychological fitness – no idleness, more reading and interaction with people. Man/woman for others. Broad outlook is essential.
c. Ethical/social fitness – be ecumenical. People expect you to be a model pastor/person.
d. Spiritual fitness – devotional life (personal and corporate)

   "You are a gift from God." I Peter 4.10, Philippians 4.19, Romans 3.24 etc

   Paul writes to Timothy: I Timothy 4.14

   Do not neglect the gift that is in you.... Pay close attention to yourself, and to your teaching, continue in these things, for in so doing this you will save both yourself and your hearers.

Timothy has been given a gift, in his case the gift to teach and to pastor. And this has been confirmed by Paul commissioning Timothy for ministry. He is not to neglect the gift, to leave it buried within, or to hide it under bushel.

It is my conviction that each preacher has a gift or more gifts.

In this context, I would like to look briefly at this passage with two questions in mind. First, why do we neglect our gifts? And second: How can we ensure that we will not neglect them but live fully and creatively, abundantly and faithfully as God's gifted ministers?

The Neglect of Our Gifts

We have the tendency to neglect or deny our primary gifts in the ministry of teaching, preaching, ministering, etc. because we think too little of them. This must have been an issue for Timothy. Everything in the college could have been very ideal like on the Mount of Transfiguration. But once you are in the field – faced with multiple situations and problems and challenges. You might think what do I have to share with the elders who have so much more wisdom than I? The author says to Timothy, do not let anyone put you down, because you are young.

Often people neglect their gifts, because of the feelings of superiority or inferiority or low self-esteem.

God calls Moses. Moses says, I am slow of speech. God calls Paul, and Paul confesses that he does not possess eloquent wisdom. Both Moses and Paul became mighty leaders in the society. Paul later in his letters he had a wonderful insight that we have the treasure of the gospel in earthen vessels (2 Cor. 4,7) He makes it clear that the power belongs to God and not to us. God wants to use ordinary people like you and me. Who else would God chose to use? God did not enter human history through kings, emperors and rulers. God came in the form of a baby, born in cattle stable and died on the cross. God can work through you. God can use you, do not neglect the call and the gift of ministry.

Strategies to keep going in the ministry. There will be times of frustration and giving up of the vigour and interest. Remember your call. Remember your training, remember your teachers. Remember your colleagues. Remember your classmates.

Firstly, live in dialogue with scriptures which show us the truth, inspiring us to live God's way. Through the word of God, we are put together and shaped up for the tasks God has for us. Through your training here, what has been hidden has been revealed. You are now equipped to go out and to serve.

Secondly, listen to your mentors in faith. For Timothy that person was Paul. Our mentors are encouragers, those men and women who see something in us. They move us forward into the painful and wondrous work of becoming who, in God's design, we are intended to be. There is often for individuals an inner sense of who we are, of what we have been created to be, and our theological training shapes and confirms it. In the Christian faith, we define a sacrament as an outward and visible sign of an inward and spiritual grace. I believe you have been prepared inwardly and spiritually. And today's valedictory service is an outward sign that your inner experience has become a reality.

Mentors do that for us. Your teachers have done it for you. Now you can do it for others.

Every pastor is a visionary of his/her church. A creative thinker, an objective analyst, positive contributor and motivator. What our teachers have done for you, you could do it for others. I am speaking at a very simple level. Encourage, affirm, uplift, strengthen and build up. We are always blessed by the touch of other persons who say, you are special, you are beloved in the right of God. And I believe in you! Mentors do this for us. And I hear Paul telling Timothy, you can do it.

Finally, the use of our gifts is an issue of profound life-altering importance for others. As you use your gifts, Paul says, you will save both yourself and your hearers. What a statement! As we use our gifts, we save ourselves and those given to our charge and affected by our ministry. Our gifts really matter to us for our own sake. Someone has put it this way: Salvation is for creation. We are saved in order to be a blessing to others, through the particular gifts that God has placed within us. And in that process, everyone becomes closer to us.

There is a treasure, a gift, within you. You are a gift from God. Do not neglect the gift that is within you. When Abraham was called – God says to him – you shall be a blessing. This is exactly what Paul writes to Timothy. Do not neglect the gift in you.

You have a call,

You have a gift

To have a call and a gift of the ministry is to receive a vision from God. When a vision is taken seriously it becomes a manifesto for action. You know the vision you have and the manifesto for implementation. Go out into the world as witnesses and servants of Christ, as bridge builders, as enablers and as path breakers.

"Called to Preach: Prophetic, Poetic and Pastoral Dimensions of the Call" (Preaching in the 21st Century, Preface."

Chapter 4

How and What was Preaching in the New Testament Times?

The New Testament consists of the Gospels and Epistles.

The Gospels are the result of the preaching of the Apostles.

The Epistles are written to churches founded by the Apostolic preaching, particularly by Paul.

The Terminology applied to Preaching is "Proclamation".

"Christian proclamation according to Paul: has the cross at its centre, as its defining point, in its message: Christ crucified, in its method: weakness; is faithful to the Gospel received in the Church; is not for gain, either financial or personal; is not dependent on eloquence, self-commendation, ancestral superiority, spiritual experience, and it bears the marks of costly service" (Preaching in the 21st Century, p. 72).

The Distinction between Teaching and Preaching – teaching is for edification and maturity and preaching is for the listening of the good news. Jesus teaches the disciples and preaches to the crowds.

The Forms of Preaching – we find a variety of methods. Parables (story telling), narration, and sayings through images.

The Contents of Preaching – Kingdom of God by Jesus Christ and Jesus and his cross and crucifixion and resurrection by the apostles. The proclaimer becomes the proclaimed.

The Preaching of John the Baptist – for repentance and preparation to enter int the kingdom of God.

The Preaching of Jesus of Nazareth – through Parables, performance of Miracles and occasional Sayings.

The Apostolic Preaching – is found in the book of the Acts of the Apostles basically by Peter, Philip, Stephen, Paul, Apollos, Timothy, and Titus and others. They concentrate on the cross and resurrection of Jesus and their own experience.

The Preaching in the Letter to the Hebrews – that Jesus is the true High Priest.

The Preaching in the Letter of James – that works is also as important as faith.

Preaching in the Letter of Revelation – new creation; new heaven and new earth.

The Theology of Preaching consists of,

Repentance

Kingdom of God

The Crucified and Resurrected Lord

The Preaching Styles/Methods

Narrative, Story Telling, Witnessing/Testimonies

Graeco-Roman Environment – public speeches of oratory

We find "High Culture" and "Strict Order".

Public Speaking and Rhetorics

The Hellenistic and Jewish Contexts

Greek Rhetoric – learned speaking.

Jewish Teaching – instruction in the Synagogues

After Reformation in the 16th, the Word became prominent.

The Established Churches and Missionary Contexts

Pastoral – to equip the members for the work of ministry.

Evangelistic – to proclaim good news to the poor.

For Further Reading

Leadership Handbooks of Practical Theology, Volume One, *Word and Worship,* General Editor, James D. Berkley, Baker Book House, Grand Rapids, Michigan, 1992.

Handbook of Contemporary Preaching, Michael Duduit, Editor, Broadman & Holman Publishers, 1992.

Concise Encyclopaedia of Preaching, William H. Willimon & Richard Lischer, editors, Westminster John Knox Press, 1995.

Stott, John. The Preacher's Portrait: Great Word Pictures from The New Testament *(Christian Classic Series).* England, InterVarsity Press, 1996.

Chapter 5

What is Preaching in the 21st Century?

A festschrift was prepared and published in 2013 by my daughter Amritha with the title, Preaching in the 21st century – towards a new Homiletics. The collection of articles from theologians, pastors, and academicians from India and across the globe reflecting on the topic of preaching in the context of technological advancement, scientific exploration, and vast social media. The book provides several insights into facing the challenges of the modern society.

The Gospel is eternal, but the proclamation varies from time to time. New situations demand new interpretation. That's why the term contextual preaching came into existence.

We find preaching based on the lectionaries among the historic churches, and free preaching in the independent churches. Storytelling, analytical or biographical or allegorical sermons are found in the free churches. Bible reference sermons are very common. They may be called reference sermons. Sometimes we find events description sermons. There are a variety of sermons these days.

Preaching in the 21st century will start by reading the gospel from the places of hurt and injustice that is so much prevalent in the society. From there, we start to make sense of the Bible and our own contexts. A sermon is to relate the text to the context. Biblical preaching is ever relevant.

Preaching in the 21st century will have to empower our spiritual lives and spiritual practices and take us to find ways and means to ring about justice which is grounded in the gospel of Jesus Christ. Preaching must be authentic addressing the issues of the community.

Preaching in the 21st century will have to make us all know the discrimination of the poor and Dalits. Preaching without pastoral concern is something lacking in the realm of Christian participation in the society.

Preaching in the 21st century will have to face a complex net of issues that are all inter-connected, the destruction of our ecology, casteism, patriarchy, militarism, domination of the rich, sexual violence, social class struggles etc. Addressing societal issues involved prophetic preaching.

Preaching in the 21st century will have to comfort the uncomfortable and make uncomfortable the comforted. Our conscience needs to be awakened once again.

All movements of faith and justice will continue to inspire us. We must engage the liturgical sources of our faith along with the thousands of other symbols of liberation around the world. We stand on ecumenical ground to be in solidarity with one another.

Preaching in the 21st century will find metaphors to continue the demand Jesus asked of Peter: Feed my sheep and from this strength we will go forward on behalf of the God who has a clear preference for the poor!

The centre of this gospel is the love of God, the redemptive gospel of Jesus Christ and the radical presence of the Holy Spirit! Otherwise, it will be preaching about us.

See, **preaching in the 21st Century, towards a new homiletics**, edited by Vinod Victor and Amritha Bosi Perumalla, ISPCK, Delhi, 2013.

Chapter 6

What are Some of the Biblical Insights for Preaching in Multi-religious Context?

These insights come out of the course I taught at San Francisco Theological Seminary to Doctorate in Ministry (D.Min) students in 1997 in San Francisco, United States.

We have seen that Christian Preaching is:

1. **Preaching within the Church**

    a. Lectionary preaching

Planned Preaching according to the seasons of the church year.

Advent, Christmas, Epiphany, Lent, Easter, Ascension, Pentecost, Trinity …

2. **Free Preaching**

Free churches and particularly Baptists and others

Free selection of biblical passages and themes

Purpose of Preaching:

Edification

Growing in Faith

Deeper Understanding of the Scriptures

Christian Living and Witnessing

And Christian Mission in different ways etc.

3. **Preaching Outside of the Church**
    a. Revival preaching
    b. Missionary preaching
    c. Evangelistic preaching
    d. Church Plantation etc.

    Purpose: Evangelization of the World

4. **Missionary Times**

Three streams:

a. Exclusive claims – that Jesus is the savior and redeemer and only revelation of God.
b. Inclusive claims – those other religions and faiths do have revelation of God.
c. Pluralistic understanding – that all religions and faiths contain eternal truth.

5. **What could be the preaching now in a secular/multi-religious and multi-cultural societies?**

    Understanding without prejudice. We need to know and understand other faiths. That's why inter-religious dialogue is emphasized.

Christian Preaching in Pluralist Context: Towards new Homiletics – A Proposal

Introduction

I am writing another book.

The book will initiate reflection on the question of the nature and the content of Christian Preaching in a multi-religious and multi-cultural context commonly called pluralist society. The world in which we live is no longer homogeneous one but a diverse entity with religions, cultures and ideologies, inspite of globalisation and internationalisation of many things through communication, travel and trade and commerce. The situation demands a reflection on the Christian preaching both in its form and content.

The book will try to discover the biblical and theological resources to understand and to propose a new homiletic for pluralist contexts.

The book will consist of four parts.

Part I: Challenges of Pastoral Ministry Today

Different Dimensions of Christian Ministry

Chances and Challenges of Christian Faith in Non-Christian Environment

Missionary Times:

Exclusive Attitude

International Mission Conference Tambaram, Chennai 1938

Christian Message in a Non-Christian World, Hendrick Kraemer

Madras Re-Thinking Group

P. Chenchiah, V. Chakkrai and E. Asirvadam and A. J. Apasamy

Partial Truth and Revelation

Robert De Nobilie

Inclusive Attitude

Pluralist Society

Inter-Religious Dialogue (WCC, Nairobi 1975)

Dialogue with People of other Faiths and Ideologies

Pre-Independence Times

Christian Missions and British Raj

Christian Missions and Muslim Rulers

Christian Thinkers

E. Stanley Jones

Round Table Conferences

Sat Tal Ashram

J. N. Farquhar, The Crown of Hinduism

Sadhu Sundar Singh, Water of life in an Indian cup

Post Independence

Indian Constitution and Its Preamble

India a Sovereign, Democratic, Socialist and Secular Republic

Minority Rights to Christians and Muslims,

Personal laws reg. marriage and property

Dalit Christians excluded from Scheduled Caste Status since 1950

Anti-Conversion Laws enacted since 1965 in States

Hindu Revival

V. P. Singh and Mandal Commission in 1988, Caste Identities

Mahabharatha TV Serial

Ramayana TV Serial

Lal Kishan Advani Rath Yatra

Demolition of Babri Majid, December 6, 1992

Bharatiya Janatha Party in Power

(Rashtriya Svayam Sevak Sang, (RSS),

Bajrang Dal,

Vishwa Hindu Parishad (VHP),

Bharatiya Janata Party, etc).

WCC General Assembly New Delhi 1961: Jesus Christ is light of the World.

P. D. Devanandan

Stanley J. Samartha

Israel Selvanayagam

The Establishment of the National Biblical Catechetical Liturgical Centre in Bengaluru (NBCLC) 1961.

Ishavani Kendra, Pune.

Indigenisation

Worship, Liturgy and Literature and Architecture, Songs, Bhajans

Art and Music (Jyothi Sahi, P. Solomon Raj, Richard Taylor et el).

Inculturation

Art, Architecture, Songs, Bhajans, Dress and Dance

Indian Christian Theology, Robin Boyd

The Acknowledged Christ of Indian Renaissance, M. M. Thomas

Dalit Theology, Indian Theology of Liberation

Current Context

The Hindu Fundamentalism, Nationalism

The Ghar Wapasi Movement

The Ghau Rakshak (Cow Protection) Movement

Ban on Beef Eating in several states

Chances

Institutions

schools, colleges, hospitals, orphanages, etc.

Religious teaching is prohibited

Free Press (Publications)

Free Media (TV)

Free Movement of people

Freedom to worship

Public meetings!

Missionaries of Charity

Kinder Not Hilfe

Bread for the World

Caritas and Misereor etc.

Red Cross

World Vision

I. I became all things to all people. St. Paul

II. All things are possible, but all things are not helpful. St. Paul

III. M. K. Gandhi, I am a Hindu, a Muslim, a Sikh, a Christian and a Buddhist

Acceptance/recognition with humility is the need of the hour.

Cooperation without compromise is a must.

Examples and Insights

Text: Genesis 1:26ff

Context: The Priestly creation account, probably redacted while in exile in Babylon Sitting in exile in a foreign land, whose inhabitants worshiped Marduk, the writers affirm the creation of all humankind in the image of God.

Every human being shares the image of God.

Text: Genesis 9:8-17

Context: Following the flood, which was God's response to humankind and its wickedness, God makes an everlasting covenant with every living creature and all flesh.

Text: Genesis 12:1-3

Context: The call of Abraham, writing of God's salvific initiative in history, the Yahwist writes of the call of Abraham as proposed for the redemption of all humankind.

God's intent is for all nations of the world to be blessed.

Text: 1 Kings 17:8-24

Context: Part of the Elijah- Elisha cycles that probably have their source from stories in the pre-721 BC Northern Kingdom. In this story the non-Jewish identity of the widow and her son are not an issue. The story illustrates God's grace and mercy also to those outside the circle of Israel.

JONAH 4:10 (The entire Book of Jonah)

God spares Nineveh.

The author of Jonah warns his readers against this intolerant attitude and sets before each of them the question of whether he or she is willing to be transformed into a servant who works to accomplish the mandates of God.

The book of Jonah is so significant for understanding the Biblical basis that God also cares the gentile people.

Matthew 8:5-15: Jesus Heals a Centurion Servant

Jesus is amazed: "in no one in Israel have I found such faith."

Matthew 15:28: the Canaanite Woman's Faith

Jesus says. "Woman, great is your faith."

Mark 7:24- 30: the Syrophoenician Woman's Faithful Persistence

Luke 7:1-10: Jesus Heals a Centurion's Servant

Jesus says: I tell you, not even in Israel have I found such faith."

Luke 9:51-56: A Samaritan Village Refuses to Receive Jesus

James and John asked, "Lord, do you want us to command fire to come down from heaven and consume them?" Jesus rebukes them. parallel - Jonah

Luke 10:25-37: Parable of the Good Samaritan

John 4:1-43: Jesus and the Samaritan Woman at the Well

Context: Jesus' conversation with the Samaritan woman at the well broke cultural protocol. Jesus words point to a time when al will worship God not in a particular place but in spirit and truth.

Acts 8:26-40: Philip and the Ethiopian Eunuch

Acts 10-34...: Gentiles hear the Good News

"God shows no partiality."

Acts 15: The Council of Jerusalem

No Extra Burdens

Acts 17 Paul in Athens

Context: The Areopagus was a place for intellectual debate and celebrates a pluralism of ideas within Athens. In this setting, Paul speaks to the Athenians, beginning with that he has observed in their context. Though the form critical genre of the speech is clearly a sermon, it is easy to imagine that the tradition lying behind the text is one of the dialogues within the Areopagus.

Text: Matthew 2:1-12

Context: Matthew's inclusion of the visit from the magi from the East makes it clear that the birth of Jesus took place within a pluralistic context. Of the many themes that this text suggests, the pilgrimage of persons form outside Judaism to seek out the baby Jesus serves as a model for how we might want to enter into the world of other faiths in order to learn and gain appreciation for them. The magi chose not to read about Jesus one day in a book. They came to see and experience firsthand themselves. The warning that comes in a dream to them in verse 12 illustrates God's salvific activity outside of Judaism.

Text: Matthew 16:13-26

Context: The setting for Jesus' questions, "Who do people say that I am?" and "who do you say that I am?" is set within Caesarea Philippi, a cosmopolitan context of true pluralism. The landscape is one of Greek pantheism and Greco-Roman commercialism. The question posed to the disciples, then, is the question that our confession of Jesus as the Christ should pose to us today. Within our global context of religious and secular pluralism, what does it mean for us to be Christian, to confess that Jesus is the Christ? Jesus' teaching of the disciples, particularly considering Peter's misunderstanding, means that as Christians we are not called to be imperialists but to follow the Christ in service, humility and sacrificial love for the sake of the world.

Text: Mark 7:24- 30

Context: Jesus is in the region of Tyre, Gentile territory. Jesus' compassion on this woman is a reminder that God's love and mercy cannot be contained to only one group of people. God's mercy is responsive to all persons in need.

Text: Luke 9:49-50

Context: Jesus' disciples are concerned that someone outside the circle is doing something supposedly only reserved for the true disciples of Jesus. Jesus' reply, "Whoever is not against you is for you." reminds us of that other faiths that seek to bring wholeness to people are friends, not enemies of Christ.

Text: Luke 10: 29-37

Context: One of the often-overlooked aspects of the parable of the God Samaritan is that it follows the lawyer's question, "What must I do to inherit eternal life?" Not only is an outsider – a Samaritan! – lifted as one who manifests the spirit of the commandment to love one's neighbor; Jesus telling this story on the heels of such a question also illustrates that "eternal life" is a gift from of God that comes to those not by their creeds but by their doing the will of God.

Text: John 3:16

Context: This text is often taken by evangelicals as a proof text. Confession of faith in Jesus as the Son of God is a pre-condition for salvation and obtaining eternal life. Certainly, the programmatic agenda of the Fourth Evangelist, writing during and to persons in a pluralistic situation, is to bring people to faith in Jesus as the Son of God (cf. John 20:30-31); however, to beat people over the head with John 3:16 as a proof text for an imperialistic Christianity is to misuse the text. The text affirms God's love for the world (κοσμος). Also, in the Gospel of John, belief is a verb. In John, there are no uses of the noun, πιστος. There are, however, ninety-eight (98!) uses of the verb, πιστευω. Belief, then, cannot be subscribing to a doctrine. Rather it is a way of life that ***believes*** that Jesus is the way, the truth and the life by following Jesus and loving the world as God loves the world in Jesus.

Text: Acts 10:34-35

Context: Following the conversation of Cornelius, Peter began to speak. His speech affirms the impartiality of God, and it also exhibits good preaching. It speaks to the listeners within the context of what they understand and believe. Studying all the sermons of Peter and Paul in Acts shows the effectiveness of preaching to persons within their own framework.

We will have to honour other people's faith and will teach us to fight for their well-being.

Some Books about Inter-religious Preaching

Israel Selvanayagam has written extensively on the subject, particularly,

Relating to People of other Faiths: Insights from the Bible, 2004; and Interreligious Life Issues: Relationship, Education, Prayer, Marriage, Funeral and Engagement, 2019.

Religions and the Bible: an agenda for evangelicals / Gordon T. Smith

- Yahweh and the gods: a theology of world religions from the Pentateuch / Ed Mathew.
- Selected perspectives on world religions from wisdom literature / Michael Pocock.
- To whom shall you compare you?': Yahweh's polemic against Baal and the Babylonian idol gods in prophetic literature / Robert B. Chisholm, Jr.

- The Contribution of the Gospels and Acts to a biblical theology of religions / William J. Larkin, Jr.
- The Apostle Paul and first century religious pluralism / Don N. Howell, Jr.
- The Contribution of the General Epistles and Revelation to a biblical theology of religions / Andreas Köstenberger.
- Christianity and the religions in the history of the church / James F. Lewis.
- Religious borrowing as a two-way street: an introduction to animistic tendencies in the Euro-North American context / A. Scott Moreau.
- The Uniqueness of Christ in mission theology / Charles Van Engen.
- Christianity as a minority religion / Larry Poston.

Chapter 7

What is Exegesis and Preaching?

According to Gerhard von Rad, a well-known German scholar and preacher, there are two general principles underlying the Christian Preaching.

1. The Biblical texts must be preached, under all circumstances and at any cost. The people for whom we have a responsibility as preachers need them for living and for dying.
2. The Biblical texts can be preached.

These should be the general principles of which every preacher should be convinced of. Otherwise preaching would be meaningless.

Both exegesis and preaching means interpretation. Scientific exegesis and scientific preaching are interpretation.

Interpretation is an appropriation of an intellectual content that is being transmitted.

No understanding is possible without some kind of appropriation.

No understanding is possible unless what is to be interpreted is applied to ourselves, unless it touches us existentially.

There is no fundamental distinction between exegesis and interpretation.

EXEGESIS: What is involved includes knowledge and mystery of a foreign language and historical setting, concentration upon the substance and respect for the word and the text, from which then grows a capacity for distinguishing this form of discourse or that.

Uncritical paraphrasing is a simple repetition of the text with a few words changed, is a very bad exegesis.

The less we keep ourselves from the text, the more we seek to approach the text with clean hands and less we interrupt the text with our questions, the more directly the text will address us.

Interpretation includes:

a. Translation. Not a single word in the ancient language exactly coincides with a corresponding word in our language. We cannot translate as though Isaiah or John spoke English or Tamil or Kannada or any of our languages. However, languages can be a unity.

   Schleiermacher once said, "Either the translator leaves the author resting peacefully in so far as possible and brings the reader to him; or he leaves the reader resting peacefully in so far as possible and brings the author to him." The former is scientific exegesis, and the latter is preaching.

   Religious generalities are one of the greatest weaknesses. The greatest discovery you must make in preaching is that the texts speak for themselves. We are dealing with that word which is sharper than the two-edged sword.

b. Textual Problems – Which is the nearest to the original text?

c. Literary Problems – What is the kind of literature we are dealing with? Oracle, narrative (redactors), sayings, parable, letter etc.

d. Theological Reflection – What is the text saying about God? About Christ? About the Holy Spirit? Etc.

e. Context of the Sermon – the Nature of the Hearers

f. Construction and Communication (Delivery)

Chapter 8

What is Preaching from the Lectionary?

Church Calendar/Christian Year

The church over the years has devised its own calendar remembering and celebrating Gods mighty acts in Jesus Christ for the salvation of the world. It is also called Liturgical Year. Christian Year that consists of Advent, Christmas, Epiphany, Lent, Holy Week, Good Friday, Easter, Ascension, Pentecost etc.) remembering the life of Christ chronologically and in order to strengthen Christian faith in God through Christ for true discipleship. Through the course of the year the whole biblical story of Jesus Christ is told in worship. The Christian year is arranged around two important festivals namely Christmas and Easter. Each is preceded by a time of preparation, reaching the climax in actual celebration of the birth of Christ and resurrection of Christ respectively.

The following of Church year or Christian year mark the journey of faith through the life of Christ. The change of colours for seasons enables worshippers to have a sense of movement because worship is dynamic and not static nor routine. In worship we are on our way to God's goal and purpose of making us mature followers of Christ and equipping us to be his witnesses in the world.

There are also some special days of thanksgiving commonly called harvest festival and days set apart for worthy causes and saints of the church. The seasons of Christian year have some parallels in the life of worshippers. The birth of Christ at Christmas reminds us that life is a gift of God, the remembering of the struggles and sorrows of Jesus at Lent, comforts our own struggles and the new life of Easter touch human experience deeply. The Christian year is not simply a progression of the events in the life of Christ, but also help us to find our own ways through the journey of faith, with faith, hope, and love).

One could consider:

1. The Lectionary – planned reading of the scripture.

   Readings from the Old Testament, Psalms, Epistle, and the Gospel.
2. Origins of Lectionary based Preaching.
3. Later Developments
4. The Reformation
5. Post Reformation Changes
6. The Common Lectionary
7. The Lectionaries of the Churches in India
8. The Church Year

   Advent, Christmas, Epiphany, Lent, Holy Week, Easter, Ascension, Pentecost, Trinity, After Pentecost, Advent …
9. The Benefits of Peaching from the Lectionary
   a. Comprehensive Planning
   b. Scriptural Comprehensiveness
   c. Scriptural Primacy
   d. Collective Possibilities
   e. Integration of Sermon and Liturgy
   f. Instructional Facility
   g. Theological Reflection
   h. Maintains good Scriptural Discipline

   i. Congregational Experience
   j. Ecumenical Sharing
   k. Christian Education
   l. Collective Study and Preparation
   m. Biblical Basis of Preaching
   n. Biblical Learning
   o. Biblical Integrity

10. Areas that Need Attention
   a. Choice of Texts for Preaching
   b. Need for Continuity
   c. Response to Circumstances
   d. Avoid Quick Conclusions
   e. Avoid Superficial Connections
   f. Quick and Superficial Decisions

a. Reading of the Bible lessons in Worship

The practice of readings varies from church to church according to their tradition.

Generally, in all constitutional churches, which are governed by a constitution, all lay are encouraged to read the lessons in worship. The lesson well-read is already half sermon preached. Clear pronunciation, reading of sentences and not just words, that make sense and carry meaning is important.

We believe in the priesthood of all believers.

However, in the Catholic and Episcopal Churches, the Gospel is read by the priest, and all are expected to stand.

As far as preaching is concerned, it depends on the preacher.

In the CSI we have a theme and corresponding four lessons.

It depends on the preacher where he or she begins and where he ends.

I generally go by the theme and take insights from the biblical texts.

We don't have time to do exegesis and exposition of the texts in the short time during worship.

As per the private or independent churches are concerned there are no fixed rules and procedures.

However, they tend to concentrate on OT because they are good story tellers.

CSI Order of Worship is well organised theologically, in a very progressive manner.

All the major elements of liturgical tradition follow one after the other in such a way the worshippers are expected and given an opportunity to experience deep spirituality at least once a week.

Well experienced liturgical scholars, men, and women of spiritual worth prepared it for the use in the congregations.

The Book of Common Worship first published in 1962, was in preparation for 15 long years by the Liturgical Committee of the Synod.

The structure is based on the Anglican Book of Common Prayer, originally in 1661, prepared by Archbishop Thomas Cranmer and others.

Main elements:

Praise and thanksgiving.

Confession of Sin and Absolution.

Reading, preaching and affirmation of faith.

Offertory,

Eucharist known as Breaking of the Bread and Sharing of the Cup.

Benediction and Commission.

Appropriate hymns are sung in between.

Some social elements like announcements are also made.

b. Vestments, Robes, and Stoles and Liturgical Colours

The clerical garments play a role not only in appearance but also in liturgy and preaching.

Vestments are special robes worn by the ordained bishops and priests and presbyters and deacons and altar servers in Christian churches. Clerical vestments, robes and stoles vary from church to church in their respective traditions. They are the ceremonial clothes, with distinctive pattern of communication of a particular meaning. They are worn to express the nature of the occasion and to distinguish the respective role and rank of each participant.

Although there are some indications of clerical dresses for the priests in the Books of Leviticus and Numbers in the Old Testament of the Bible, one should not draw a conclusion that what we have today in the form of vestments, robes and stoles in the church are drawn from the Old Testament. Our clerical robes are much more evolved from the Western churches than derived from the Bible in the post Constantine era when church became an official organisation or institution in the end of the 4th and beginning of the 5th century AD.

St. Jerome (341–420) distinguishes between everyday clothing and a special suit of clean clothes for wearing in the church (See J. G. Davies, p. 523). We have inherited from the Western churches as they evangelized us and established churches in India. The New Testament does not give any importance nor prescribe any ecclesiastical clothing except a few references here and there (See St. Mathew 5.40 coat, St. John 19.23 seamless tunic worn by Jesus, Revelation 1.13 a visionary person robed to his feet). For an elaborate description of vestments of churches, see Gilbert Cope article in, A New Dictionary of Liturgy and Worship, edited by J. G. Davies, SCM Press 1986, pp. 521 to 540.

1. Ecclesiastical/Church Traditions

There are some major traditions of the One, Holy, Catholic and Apostolic Church in the world. There are also some churches or denominations that may not fall under any category such as

Seventh Day Adventists, Church of Jesus Christ of the Latter-Day Saints (also known as Mormons), Jehovah Witnesses, the Scientologists and Quakers. However, one can trace at least four major streams of Christian faith traditions.

A. The Eastern Orthodox Churches (Armenian, Greek, Russian, Syrian, Chaldean, Ethiopian, Coptic (Egyptian) and Rumanian). These are the ancient churches that got separate status and identities after the great ancient Church Councils of Nicaea 325 AD, Constantinople 381 AD, Ephesus 431 AD, Chalcedon 451 AD, which debated the true nature of Christs humanity and divinity. Eastern Churches generally tend to emphasize the humanity of Christ, whereas the Roman Catholic Church commonly called the Western Church emphasizes the divinity. Jerusalem, Alexandria in Egypt, Antioch in Syria, Constantinople, and Rome are the ancient centres of Christianity which preserved the liturgy and worship of the Apostolic and post apostolic times in Greek, Armenian, Syrian Coptic and Latin languages. These are the churches that celebrate the divine liturgy. (See, Serget Hackel, Orthodox Worship, in J. G. Davies, A New Dictionary of Liturgy and Worship, pp. 421 to 423). We have in India, the Malankara Orthodox Syrian church, the Indian Orthodox church, the Chaldean Syrian Church, Armenia church, Jacobite Syrian Orthodox church, and the Mar Thoma churches identified as Orthodox churches. What is common to them is the St, James ancient liturgy, believed to have been written by James, the brother of Jesus who presided the Jerusalem Council (see Acts of the Apostles, chapter 15).

B. The Roman Catholic Church. It is traced back to St, Peter and St. Paul wrote one of his profound theological epistles to the church there, called the Epistle to the Romans. The church in Rome became strong and popular as the Roman empire embraced it as official religion at the time of Constantine the emperor in 4th century. After the Reformation of the 16th century, Roman Catholic Church became an entity by itself as the church was divided into many reformed denominations beside the Catholic. It is the largest wing of the one, holy, catholic, and apostolic church.

C. The Reformed Western Churches commonly known as the Major Protestant Churches (The Church of England, The Reformed Church (Presbyterian Churches, the Congregationalists), the Evangelical Lutheran Churches, the Baptist Churches, the United Churches (Church of South India, Church of North India), The Methodist Churches (British Wesleyan Methodist, the American Methodist, the Mennonite Church etc.)

D. Pentecostal/Charismatic free or independent churches (Brethren Groups, Hebron Churches, Indian Pentecostal Churches, Evangelical Churches, Bible Mission Church etc). These are faith communities that came about in 20th century and continues to grow in every place. They are free and are not confined to any tradition and normally do not use any religious vestments except white dress.

The Eastern Orthodox churches and the Roman Catholic churches use vestments, clerical robes, vestures and stoles extensively as the occasions demand on Sundays and on all liturgical occasions.

2. There are Four Types of Ecclesiastical Robes

a. the garments that are worn for the Eucharist and other sacramental ceremonies.

b. the garments that are used at other liturgical occasions (worship of various types).

c. there are various items of clothing that indicate rank and role of specific orders of ordained men and women.

d. the garments which are clerical in nature by worn by non-clerics like choir etc.

3. The Protestant churches that came out as separate churches after the Reformation of Martin Luther in Germany, John Calvin in Geneva, Huldrich Zwingli in Zurich in Switzerland, John Knox in Scotland, John Wesley and Charles Wesley in England and others like King Henry VIII who separated Church of England from the Roman Catholic Church in the 16th century in Europe, strongly opposed ornate architecture and colourful clerical vestments. They considered them as distraction from the main emphasis in worship, namely proclamation of God's word and administration of the sacraments of Baptism and Holy Communion. The elaborate and excessive ceremonial colourful robes in the Middle Ages seemed to have distracted from worship of true God to the celebrants of the sacraments and leaders/clergy of the worship.

4. The German Evangelical Lutheran churches reduced the clerical robes to plain black robes which they continue even today. The Reformed and Methodist Churches switched over to white robes and brought visual focus on to the open Bible and Lords Supper, also called Eucharist or Holy Communion. The English Puritans under the leadership of Oliver Cromwell in the 17th century made things much simpler both in architecture and in the clerical robes. They vehemently opposed to any colourful character of worship, including stopping of the celebration of Christmas.

In the course of time some of the Protestant churches started reclaiming some clerical traditions thinking that colours and symbols can be good aids for meaningful worship.

Different vestments are prescribed and used for different ceremonies or formal observance with rules and established customs. They are called rite or ritual in worship.

Generally white robes are considered appropriate for worship. However, the focus continues to be on preaching among the churches that came out of Reformation of the 16th century in Europe and 18th century in United Kingdom.

5. The Pastoral Offices in the Church of South India

a. Bishop: The word Bishop is a translation of the Greek word Episkopos, meaning overseer or supervisor. The chief priest of a diocese and is responsible for the pastoral care his or her diocese. In the early church the one who was called Bishop was the main leader at worship and pastoral care of the congregation. Later the role became that of a priest with administrative responsibilities over a group of churches within a geographical area called a diocese. (See CSI Constitution, chapter on Ministry of the Church).

At the time of the ordination/consecration as a Bishop, he or she is given the certain things as signs and symbols of his/her ministry as can be seen below.

Bishop: overseer of the diocese with pastoral care and concern, especially of the clergy and their families.

Expected to be chief shepherd of the people that they may not to go astray but lead them to and in green pastures of spirituality.

He and his family are first servants of the diocese they serve, setting an example for another clergy.

He or she is basically a teacher of faith and preacher of the gospel, and trainer of the clergy.

b. Presbyter: The word Presbyter is a translation of the Greek word Presbyteros, meaning and elder. The Presbyterian church continues to use it for their pastors. The CSI adopted this use for its priests which can be seen as an influence from the Presbyterian churches that have joined union in 1947 (See CSI Constitution, chapter on Ministry of the Church).

The CSI has deliberately used presbyter instead of priest as in Anglican, Orthodox and Roman Catholic Churches not only because the Presbyterians joined the union but also for theological reasons. A priest is one who conducts religious rites or rituals in a church as per specifications according to rules and regulations. A priest has the connotation as a pujari who does certain rituals. But a presbyter being an elder, is more than a priest. He or she is a preacher, enabler, coordinator, and teacher etc. The Church of England has a hierarchical set of priests, namely Curate, Priest, Canon, Dean, Arch – deacon, Suffragan Bishop, Assistant Bishop, Diocesan Bishop, Archbishop and Primate. CSI gave up such hierarchy of priests and retained only three, namely Bishops, Presbyters and Deacons. Sometimes it appears that such simplification has lost incentives for the incumbent clergy.

Presbyter: priest and chief elder in the church devoting his time for the ministry of preaching and celebration of sacraments of the church. A person with spiritual responsibility of the pastorate in his charge.

c. Deacon: The word deacon comes from the Greek word Diaconate, meaning the one who serves. It is an office in the churches like Anglican, Orthodox and Roman Catholic and in the CSI, under the priest or presbyter. He or she is the one who assists at liturgical ceremonies at worship and at the altar. They also assist the senior clergy in pastoral work, administrative committees of a Protestant church. In the CSI it is beginning of the Christian ministry in a diocese. However, it should not be seen as a steppingstone before becoming a presbyter as it is generally understood. The deacon is one traditionally who is to help in the worship, care for the needy particularly orphans and widows. It is an office of service.

Whether Bishop, or Presbyter or Deacon, they all have one common thing of service to God through the ministry of the church. The motto being "the servants of the servant Lord" as presented by the Pastoral Aid Department of the CSI.

In the threefold ministry of the CSI, the Bishops, the Presbyters, and the Deacons constitute a hierarchy of sharing the ministry of the church.

Besides the Bishops, Presbyters and Deacons, we also have CSI Order of Sisters who are unmarried and dedicated to prayer, meditation, and service lifelong. They too have a vestment. It is blue saree with a white or black border.

The Evangelists, called paid lay workers, in the diocese are expected to use white dress while doing liturgical service.

There is no dress code prescribed for the lay leaders who participate in worship through offering of prayers or reading of the Bible lessons.

A brief time of quietness in between the major elements of worship for personal prayer and reflection.

Responsive reading of the psalm appears to be a mere routine.

People should reflect and digest the content of the psalm.

What matters is not the length of worship but quality of spirituality.

Visitors and guests are welcomed at the time of announcements, but I wish they be invited to stand so that others can see and stay back after worship that the pastor and church elders may meet them.

Worship is not a routine ritual but a spiritual experience both individually and collectively.

Members who are unable to walk up to the altar may be advised to sit either in the front row or back row so that they may be administered elements of bread and wine together rather than spread across the whole church.

Some people still sit and pray at the end of the service.

Others may be advised to leave quietly and engage in their conversations outside.

Worship is also a time of fellowship with one another, rather than rushing home immediately, unless necessary.

Members should also interact with the pastor and preacher of the day after worship.

Creativity in prayers, sermon, and other various activities be encouraged.

Sister: a woman of the church completely dedicated to the ministry of prayer, meditation and service in orphanages, hostels, retreat centres, and care of the widows and other needy persons.

The sisterhood in the CSI was started by a Methodist Missionary lady by name Carol Graham. She also established CSI Women's Fellowship in 1948.

Vishranti Nilayam Bengaluru is the headquarters for both CSIWF and CSI Order of Sisters. It has a beautiful chapel and Sister house.

Sister Woolard was an outstanding CSI Sister for many years. Recently the sisterhood has declined in numbers.

6. Clerical Vestments of the Church of South India

By and large Church of South India has adopted the clerical robes of the Church of England since they joined the union in 1947 and continues to have a major influence in worship and other liturgical practices. The Church of England in India then was called Church of India, Burma, and Ceylon. However, the use of certain robes like alb, mitre (cap), chasuble (colourfully decorated tent like shape gown according to the season of the year, worn on top of the cassock), chimere (black or red over alb worn above the cassock etc) was discontinued after the Union. The Church of England, commonly called Anglican church has many more types of clerical supplements, like cope, tippet, hood, almuce etc. White cassocks both for Bishops and presbyters and deacons are prescribed in the CSI.

a. Cassock. The word cassock is derived from Italian word cassaca, worn in the ancient world. A cassock is a full-length close-fitting robe for use by the priests and other clerics. It may be also worn by the members of the choir. The colour and pattern differ from tradition to tradition.

b. Girdle. Usually, a girdle is worn around the waist on top of the cassock, black for the presbyters and velvet colour for the bishops. They are to confine the loose and flowing outer robes as to allow freedom of movement. Biblically and theologically, they represent the attitude of service. (See St. Johns Gospel 13, Jesus at the time of washing the disciple's feet in Upper Room).

c. Surplice. On top of the cassocks the priests would have a surplice in white. It is a white fabric or other colours with wide sleeves worn over the cassock. However, the Bishops would have saffron bands or slips at the end of the arms of the surplice along with orange stoles. The bishops are expected to use the same surplice called rochet and the stoles throughout the year as a sign and symbol of continuity in ministry. A stole is a liturgical vestment worn around the neck by all ordained ministers. Normally a 4" (inches) broad long cloth usually crafted in the colour of the day or season, often bearing symbols appropriate to the day or season. It is worn over the shoulders of those who are ordained as priests or presbyters or deacons to the pastoral office. There is a difference the way deacons use the stole. A deacon wears a stole as a sash over the left shoulder fastening or looping below the right arm. It is put across the shoulder as a sign of service and presbyters use straight around the back of the neck, as a sign and expression that he or she is a fully ordained minister.

d. Stole. Whereas the presbyters and deacons change the stoles of different colours according to the season of the Christian Year, the Bishops in the CSI wear the same stoles throughout the year. The stoles are usually velvet, white, green and black for the presbyters and deacons as the occasion or season demands.

Church of South India not only simplified clerical vestments but also clerical orders. Our clerical vestments consist of white cassock, girdle, surplice, stoles of different colours as occasion demands to all presbyters and deacons. At the time of ordination either as presbyter or deacon, the Bible is given with the commission to study, teach and preach the word of God. (See CSI Constitution chapter on Ministry of the Church and the form of ordinal in the Book of Common Worship). However, Bishops are given in addition to the Bible, a rochet, a cross and a staff and a ring, signifying various aspects of the episcopal office and duties. A constitution of the CSI and or of the diocese are also handed over at the time of the consecration as Bishop of the Church of South India and installation as a Bishop in a particular diocese. A Bishop is a Bishop of the CSI but in office in a particular diocese. That is why a Bishop is addressed as Bishop in Medak, or in Karimnagar, or in Dornakal, or in Rayalaseema, in Nandyal, in Krishna Godavari etc. Likewise, in the dioceses across Tamil Nādu, Karnataka, Kerala, and Jaffna in Sri Lanka of the CSI.

e. Rochet, an ancient form of alb or surplice with narrow sleeves used by priests. However, in the course of time it became the prerogative of bishops, cardinals, and canons. It is, as adopted by the CSI, a kind of distinction from the presbyters with saffron endings to coincide with the religious ethos of the ancient India.

f. Cross as constant reminder of the ministry of Christ. Originally it was meant to be a wooden cross, symbolising the simplicity of service. Consciously golden cross was given up embracing the poverty of the people of God. There are Bishops who consciously wear only wooden cross. After the formation of the Church of South India much of the paraphernalia regarding the vestments and addressing the bishops as "my lord" etc. was discontinued and the office of the bishop was redefined as leader of evangelism, teacher, and pastor (See for further discussion on the subject, Bishop Lesslie Newbigins article, The Other Side of 1947, in Greater Peace, Closer Fellowship, Fuller Life, CSI Golden Jubilee Publication 1997, pp. 1 to 7.

g. Staff, as a sign and symbol of the shepherding role of the bishop as the chief pastor of the diocese.

h. Ring, traditionally interpreted as being wedded to Christ (purely Western concept) but today we might say that a ring is a sign and symbol of the bishops love for his/her diocese and its people, and vice versa as it is presented by the diocese.

i. Constitution since the bishop functions within the parameters set by the Constitution of the CSI as well as his/her diocese.

j. Clerical shirts and collars. A new development in the last 25 to 30 years is the use of clerical shirts and clerical collars by the clergy. Velvet colour shirts by the bishops and different coloured shirts by the clergy with white plastic slips. Sometimes white clerical collars are used round the neck. This is certainly an influence from the Anglican Church in England as our clergy and Bishops are exposed to their clerical garments especially at Lambeth Conference of the Bishops. Some Bishops began to use even chimere and mitre contrary to CSI established practices of only rochet and stole.

7. The significance of the clerical vestments lies as a means of communication, both liturgical and theological and sometimes even political, social, and personal. Signs and symbols and colours can mean many things to many people according to the cultural context. As it has been said that the beauty is in the eye of the beholder. Some find it extremely useful, and others find them as hindrance. Vestments can speak for themselves at times.

Most churches, at least in urban areas have a room called Vestry where the clergy and the choir may dress up their vestments. The vestry is also called sacristy. Clerical vestments are not meant for show but for service in the liturgical ministry of the church. Thus, they should not be misused or overused. They need to be always kept clean and tidy. Presbyters and deacons are not supposed to run around with surplice and stole on. They may always have cassock on but not surplice and stole when not in worship.

8. Liturgical Colours

Although early church preferred white for liturgical dress, other colours gradually came into use in the course of time.

White the colour of joy and purity is used for the seasons of Christmas and Easter. Red, which is the colour of blood, is used in some churches like the Church of North India on days when we remember the passion of Jesus Christ on Passion Sunday and Good Friday. Red is also used on the day of Pentecost to symbolise the coming of the Holy Spirit as of Fire. Green as seen everywhere in plants and trees symbolizes life and hope and it is used mostly between Christmas and Easter, commonly known as ordinary time (See CSI Lectionary/Almanac each year for the use of colours in the church according to the time of the Christian year).

Development of Liturgy and Liturgical Practices in the Church – An Excurse

1. The Jewish Background

   Worship at Shrines

   Temple worship

   The Sacrifices

   The chanting of Torah and Writings

   The Development of worship in Synagogues in Exile

   The reading of the Law and Prophets

   The chanting of the Psalms

   The teaching of the Rabbis
2. The Early Church, Acts 2.42
3. Traces of worship practices in Pauline Letters

   Ephesians 5.19-20, Colossians 1.15ff, I Timothy 3.16, Philippians 2.1-10
4. The Orthodox Tradition of Liturgy

   Coptic in Alexandria, Syrian in Antioch, Hebrew/Jewish in Jerusalem

   Eastern Tradition – St. James Liturgy – The Qurbana (Offering)

The Anaphora (Greek, Thanksgiving)

The Mass (Western in Rome, Thanksgiving

Mostly readings and chanting).

5. The Development of Western Liturgy

   Singing of the hymns and organ music

   Responsive reading of the Psalms

   Preaching of the Word

6. Lectio-Divina (Divine Lectionary), planned reading of the scripture (Almanac)

7. Church Year – Recollecting the greatest or mighty acts of God

   Advent to Advent _ Christian Year

   Advent and Christmas

   Epiphany

   Lent – Ash Wednesday to Palm Sunday

   Holy Week or Passion week

      Palm Sunday

      Holy Monday

      Holy Tuesday

      Holy Wednesday

      Maundy Thursday

      Good Friday

      Holy/Silent Saturday

      Easter/Day of Resurrection

      Ascension

      Pentecost

      Trinity

8. Order of Worship

   General Main elements

a. Adoration – Praise and Thanksgiving
b. Absolution – Confession of sins and absolution (Forgiveness)
c. Exposition – Reading of the Word and Preaching of the Word
d. Affirmation – Confession of Faith through Creeds
e. Offertory – of Tithes and Prayers
f. Benediction and Commission

9. Order of Worship of Eucharist in the Church of South India

   CSI Book of Common Worship 1962, an effort of the united Church

   It has roots in Christian Tradition and Wings in India (Indigenous elements)

   Roots – Anglican, Presbyterian, Congregational, Methodist elements

   Wings – Indigenous – Bhajans, lyrics, music, etc

   Renewal of Liturgy 1985 Alternate services

   Lectionary – Joint Liturgical Commission of CSII, CNI, and Mar Thoma churches

   Experimental Services at Theological colleges and Synod meetings and conferences

10. Recent Developments

    Introduction of Praise and worship

    Free Preaching and Testimonies

    Fellowship and Meals

    Use of Mass Media

    Live broadcasting on Online

Chapter 9

What are Some of the Sermon Preparation Plans?

Primarily we begin with two or three ways.

1. Inductive Method – we begin with specifics and move on to general.
2. Deductive Method – We begin with general and move and to the specific.
3. Inter-active – we engage the congregation (listeners in a dialogue by asking questions or inviting comments).

(The following plans are as suggested by the Professor Dr. John Skoglund, California, 1975 and now stands revised).

Sermon Preparation Plan – I

1. Scriptural passage on which sermon is to be based.
2. Bibliography – Books which bear directly on sermon preparation: Lexicons, concordance, wordbooks, commentaries, other biblical books, books, articles etc.
3. Context of the scriptural passage – historical, literary, other relational situations.

4. Any special critical or theological problems in relation to the passage.
5. Key words and their meanings as found in lexicons, wordbooks, and commentaries.
6. Exegesis of the passage using the best helps available.
7. Key verse or verses of the passage.
8. Theme(s) of the passage.
9. Life situation – To what special problem(s) or human situation(s) does the passage point.
10. Theme of the sermon – This should be based on the scripture passage and directed toward the life situation.
11. Proposition or Thesis of the sermon - State in one sentence what you are trying to do in this sermon.
12. Illustrations – Seek examples that illumine your theme and the points which you are making.
13. Preaching Outline – Develop a detailed outline that can be used as the basis for preaching the sermon.
14. Written manuscript - Using your outline write out your sermon in full.
15. Read the manuscript over enough so that it becomes familiar.
16. Determine the method to be used in presenting the sermon – monologue, dialogue, drama, discussion, story- telling, group discussion and other usages.
17. Use the Outline for preaching.

Sermon Preparation Plan – II

I. The World

   1. State clearly the situation, issue, problem.
   2. Seek models and analogies in literature, history, and life.
   3. Give a clear sociological, psychological, philosophical, or ethical analysis of the situation, issue, or problem.
   4. State situation, issue, or problem as a thematic question

II. The Word

1. Seek Biblical materials which deal with the situation etc, there may be themes running through the whole Bible or books, e.g., love etc.
2. If a text, make a historical, critical as well as exegetical and word study.
3. If a theme from the whole or part of the Bible, show how the theme is truly representative of the Biblical thought and not a theme imposed upon the Bible.
4. Write a summary statement of the Biblical theme.

III. The World and the Word

1. Show points of contact between the Biblical material and the situation etc.
2. Write your own answer to the issue as based upon I and II.
3. State your answer in a thesis (proposition) of one sentence.

IV. The Sermon

1. Raise the Issue: Use questions, illustrations, analogies etc.
2. Put the issue to the Biblical material.
3. Bring the issue and the Biblical material before the congregation for decision or discussion. Do not give final answers, but raise questions and challenges etc.

V. The Sermon Delivery

1. Determine the method to be used in presenting the sermon – monologue, dialogue, drama, discussion, storytelling, group discussion and other usages.
2. Develop a plan or outline of the sermon.

Sermon Preparation Plan – III

1. The context of the Biblical passage – social, political, ecclesial etc. A careful reading of the text is necessary.
2. Exegesis of the passage – translation, text variations, word study, the literary form, linguistic structure etc. Study of

the text in the light of the historical criticism i.e., problems related to textual variations, redactors intentions etc. help in understanding the text.

3. Systematic Theological Reflection – What does the passage say about God, Jesus Christ, Holy Spirit, Church, Salvation, etc. Reflection on the text theologically would mean trying to understand what it meant to the original readers in their faith and practice of the Christian life.
4. Context of the Sermon – Situation/nature of the hearers. Sitz im Leben of the listeners of the sermon.
5. Homiletic Reflection – What does it mean for us here and now? Think of the possible interpretations in the situation of the hearers for application and follow up.
6. Think of the possible analogies, illustrations, metaphors, figures of speech etc. for the illustration of the sermon.
7. Text of the sermon – fully written.
8. Plan of presentation – How the sermon is going to be preached? Determine the method to be used in presenting the sermon – monologue, dialogue, drama, discussion, storytelling, group discussion and other usages.
9. Develop a plan or outline of the sermon.

Chapter 10

What are Thematic Sermons?

1. The Preacher should know the theme thoroughly.
   - Reading on the subject
   - Observations on the subject
   - Thinking on the subject
   - Gathering materials on the subject
2. The theme should be readily understood by the congregation.
   - Arrangement of the subject matter.
     - o One theme
     - o Logical connection and sequence between the divisions
     - o Proper emphasis on various parts of the sermon
   - Introduction
     - o To awake an interest in the theme
     - o To prepare the congregation for what is to follow.
   - Sources of introduction
     - o Text
     - o The context of the sermon

    - The historical setting of the passage
    - The geographical setting
    - The customs and manners
  - Sources of conclusion
    - Story or illustration
  - Body of the sermon
    - Logical divisions
    - Progression of thought
    - Natural sequence etc.

3. The theme should not be made to appear very trivial.
4. The preacher needs to have a definite purpose in the treatment of the theme.
5. The theme should be suitable to the time, place, and occasion.

Chapter 11

What are Textual Sermons?

This form of the sermon is based on a short portion of the scripture. It involves choosing an appropriate text (a text from the lectionary). Then one needs to investigate and analyse the text to get the message it conveys. Then present it in an orderly and progressive manner that is easy for the hearers to assimilate.

1. Choice of the text
    a. Lectionary
    b. Freely chosen.
2. Length of the text
    a. Pericope
    b. Complete in conveying the meaning.
3. Advantages of having a text
    a. It awakens interest of the congregation.
    b. It gains confidence of the congregation.
    c. It gives authority and boldness to the preacher.
    d. It will keep the mind of the preacher from wandering.
    e. It will keep the preacher Biblically based.

4. Principles that govern the choice of the text
    a. The preacher must carefully consider the spiritual needs of the people to whom one is ministering.
    b. The preacher must carefully consider the season in the Christian year.
    c. The preacher must carefully consider his/her ability to deal with the text.
5. Principles that govern the preparation of the sermon
    a. Familiarity with the word by constant reading
    b. The use of notebook should be cultivated.
    c. The reading of good books provides rich material.
    d. Prayer and meditation for guidance of the Holy Spirit
6. Interpretation of the text
    a. The preacher must ascertain whether the language of the text is literal or figurative e.g., John 2.19, 21-22; Mt. 26.26-27; Mk. 14.22-24; Lk. 22.19-20; I Cor. 11.23-26; I Cor 6.11. etc.
    b. The preacher should ascertain the meaning of the words used by the writer of the passage. e.g., Faith – Gal. 1.23; I Tim. 3.9; Acts 24.24 - faith in Christ.

        But in Acts 17.31 – it is assurance.

        Flesh – Ezek. 11.19 used in contrast to stone.

        John 1.14, Rom.1.3, 9.3 refers to human nature.

        Salvation – Ex. 14.13 – deliverance; James 5.15 – bodily healing; Rom. 13.11 – whole of blessing in Christ, Heb. 2.3 – gospel.
    c. The preacher should consider the circumstances peculiar to the writer and the readers.
    d. The preacher should compare scripture with scripture. e.g., Prov. 6.14 comp. with Psalm 145.9; Ezek. 18.23 comp. II Pet. 3.9.

e. The preacher should know the manners and customs of the original readers and authors. See Job 24.16; Ezek. 12.5; Mt. 6.19; comp. Dt. 22.8 I Sam. 9.25; II Sam. 11.2; Isa. 22.1; Mk. 2.4; 13.15; and Acts 10.9.

Chapter 12

What is the Art of Communicating a Sermon?

The sermon is a creative piece of art. The ancient Greeks and Romans gave great importance to public oratory. There were schools of public speaking for them. Cicero, one of the great Greek thinkers and philosophers propounded the principles of public speaking which became classical rhetoric among the Greeks and Romans and later also among the Christian preachers.

The principles are:

1. Invention – It is getting an idea or the meaning or the message from the exegesis of a text.
2. Disposition – It is the arrangement or putting together the idea or the message.
3. Style – It is the communicative style of the speaker. It is in fact the whole personality of the speaker.
4. Memory – It is the skill to hold the content and the form together.
5. Delivery – It is the act of speaking the sermon.

These are not independent steps but interlocking process of preparation, construction, and delivery of a sermon.

Any sermon or a public speech consists of two basic components – the form and content. Our Christian preaching consists of both its form of presentation and its content. Very often preachers concentrate more on the content than on the form. The form (the way the sermon is structured and delivered) is as important as the content (the message or the gospel).

The form of the sermon includes:

a. Its structure (the beginning, the development, and the end) developing the thoughts in an orderly manner that the audience can easily follow its progression.

b. Its language and expression (the way the word/the kind of words, expressions and conceptions and the construction of sentences are used.

c. and the personality of the preacher (the style of delivery, mannerisms, and the presentation of oneself before the hearers, i.e., the congregation).

Communication takes place not only through words but through the whole personality of the speaker. Not only what is spoken but how it is spoken is important. It is here the modern communicative insights help Christian preachers tremendously.

Principles of public speaking such as:

a. good breathing

b. articulation of speech

c. variety of the pitch of the voice

d. speed of delivery

e. volume of delivery

f. pausing

g. repetition etc.

are very important. All these can be achieved through the discipline of practising. Not many are born orators, but many become effective by their constant practice. One of the popular preachers Gerald Rowlands suggests for effective communication of the sermon: "Be yourself, forget yourself, do not develop a religious voice, do not speak too softly, do not shout, dress appropriately, learn to stand properly, learn to move naturally establish and maintain eye contact" (Gerald Rowlands, A simple Guide to Preaching, p. 22).

Practice makes one perfect.

Chapter 13

What is Authority, Theology, and Importance of Christian Preaching?

Let us explore the power and authority of the Pulpit and Preacher, the underlying theological basis, and the very importance of the sermon in the context of Christian worship.

God has been using preaching (prophetic exhortation) in the OT times and Christian preaching in various forms since the NT times. Exhortation took place in the Temple, in the Synagogues and in the house gatherings. Christian preaching and proclamation have been taking place in the history of the church in many contexts/places and in different forms. Once the congregations became organised institutions and built places of worship, they began to have separate place and desks for reading the scripture and delivering the sermon. The former came to be known as lectern (reading desk) and later as pulpits (elevated platform) to address the congregations. In most established/historic churches this is the norm. Thus, the pulpit became an important instrument in the interpretation of the scripture to the church.

I. Power of the Pulpit

The power of the pulpit is the power of the gospel.

"For I am not ashamed of the gospel; it is the power of God for salvation to everyone who has faith, to the Jew first and also to the Greek." Romans 1.16.

The power of the pulpit lies not in banging or shouting but in the authority of the Word with conviction. Conviction is possible when the Spirit is at work in preaching. Hearers can easily discern who is preaching with power and who is not.

The authority of the spoken word comes from the authority of the written Word through the communication or proclamation of the preacher. Effective communication is not only the right way of speech but also the right way of interpretation of the Word.

Power of pulpit is power to change. Power of the pulpit is based on the authority of the Word. The authority of the Word is revealed in its right contextual and theological understanding and interpretation. Right interpretation is possible only with the right use of the tools of interpretation with the guidance of the Holy Spirit. Exegesis and interpretation are pre-requisites for right interpretation.

Power and Authority

There is no one definition of the authority of the preaching. It depends on the church tradition, denomination, the experience of the preacher and theological understanding. Different congregations vary in acknowledging the authority of the pulpit according to the kind of preaching and preacher. David L. Bartlett describes six types of combinations for preaching. (David L. Bartlett, Authority, Concise Encyclopaedia of Preaching, eds William H. Willimon and Richard Lischer, Westminster Press 1995, pp. 22-23).

1. Preaching has authority because it interprets the scripture. The authority of preaching is warranted by the authority of the divine Word, not necessarily to affirm any doctrine of inspiration. "The Bible is God's gift to illumine human lives, the human condition, the promise of redemption

that can comfort and urge on us." p. 22-23. Karl Barth represented such understanding.

2. The preaching has authority because it represents a pastoral word suited to the real needs of the congregation. "This kind of authority seems especially well suited to preaching based in a committed, ongoing pastoral relationship between the preacher and the people" (p. 23). The best model here is S. Paul and his relationship through his letters with the congregations he established that deal with issues of faith and practice.
3. The preaching has authority because of its place in liturgy and worship where the Word is proclaimed, and the sacraments are celebrated by the people of God. The sixth chapter of St. Johns Gospel gives an example of such combination of word and sacrament.
4. The preaching has authority because it is intellectually compelling. The preacher is not only interpreter but also commentator on contemporary life. The book of Proverbs and Wisdom literature in the Bible provide as examples.
5. The preaching has authority because of the integrity of the preacher who is a spiritual guide to the congregation. Preacher's authority depends upon the life that he lives as an example.
6. The preaching has authority because of the rhetorical power of the preacher. This is very much evident these days. This gift of effective speaking varies from preacher to preacher.

Above all, "the authority of preaching resides in the community to whom the sermon is addressed, in its texts, history, liturgy, values, and corporate life. The preacher exercises the authority of the pulpit in organic connection to scripture, teaching, presiding in liturgy, pastoral care, prophetic leadership, and daily life among the people" (Charles Rice, Authority of the Preacher, in the New Interpreters Handbook of Preaching, p. 219).

II. Theology of Preaching

"*For Jews demand signs and Greeks desire wisdom, but we proclaim Christ crucified, a stumbling block to the Jews and foolishness to the Gentiles, but to those who are the called, both Jews and Greeks, Christ the power of God and the wisdom of God.*" 1 Cor. 1.22-24

Theology of preaching is concerned with role and place of preaching in the life and ministry of the church. It must deal with theological issues like incarnation, revelation, ecclesiology, sociology, missiology, soteriology and liturgy and sacraments. There are also issue issues like authority of the preacher, the relationship of preaching to the Bible and the context of preaching. The end purpose of Christian preaching, i.e., the expectations vary from church tradition to church tradition. They include sanctification of the believers, justification of the people of faith, maturity, and growth in faith and above all salvation and new life. Christian preaching exhorts the members of the church to live according to the word preached and heard and bear witness to Jesus Christ in the world. Much of the theological activity of the church takes place in preaching. Therefore, sound theological training and ministerial formation for the work of a preacher are necessary. There are innumerable untrained preachers now in India and no wonder there are many more church groups with different theological inclinations than before and perhaps more than in any other country. Spirit blows where it will (St. John 3) but at the same time, God is God of order and discipline (1 Cor. 14).

Different emphasis is laid by different preachers and theologians on preaching. For influential Protestant theologian Friedrich Schleiermacher, preaching is to help the hearers to experience God (David M. Greenhow, Concise Encyclopaedia of Preaching p. 479). It raises God consciousness in the believers." Preaching awakens the experience of the divine" (p. 479). It is more of the subjective experience.

Over against this, the position of the well-known systematic theologian Karl Barth is that of the objective character of the Christian preaching. What is more important is Gods revelation and God speaking. This is described as *God's human speech* by Charles Bartow of Princeton. According to Barth, God's revelation takes place in three ways of the word: "the word proclaimed by the church, the word witnessed in the scripture and the word revealed in Jesus and the history of Israel" (p. 479).

For Barth preaching is not stating the meaning of the Bible, but is itself revealing the word of God, because in the very human words of preaching, God is speaking (Ibid). The ground of preaching is none other than the revelation which God has addressed to us in scripture (See Contemporary Preaching, p. 20).

For Jürgen Moltmann, Gustavo Gutierrez and other liberation theologians and preachers Christian preaching is not merely uncovering the scriptures but pointing to something new in the future, *eschaton*. The Bible promises a very hopeful future beyond the current suffering. "The good news of the gospel, the coming reign of God, is to be wrought in the gifts of life for the dying, bread for the hungry, freedom for the imprisoned. Unless the preaching of the church is spoken in the concrete realities of the everyday for the poor and oppressed, it is a false hope" (p. 480).

For African American preachers like Henry Mitchell Cleophus La Rue and others preaching it is declaring the gospel in the language and culture of the people (See Henry Mitchell, How Shall they Hear?). Preaching should reach out to people from Sunday worship to everyday life. Preaching needs to deal with everyday life of the needs of the people (p. 481).

Preaching in the Catholic church has emphasized on sanctification traditionally. However, after Vatican II, there has been a shift from sanctification to justification. Theologians and preachers like Karl Rahner, Hans Küng and Edward Schillebeeckx have provided philosophical and theological basis for a new understanding of preaching.

III. Importance of Sermon

"... I solemnly urge you, proclaim the message; be persistent whether the time is favourable or unfavourable, convince, rebuke and encourage, with the utmost patience in teaching" 2 Tim. 4.2-3.

As it has been seen before, Christian preaching finds its sanctity in the context of worship. "A sermon is an oral interpretation of scripture, usually in the context of worship. Sermons are interpretations of scripture. Communities of faith employ and acknowledge other forms of edifying discourse, but a sermon properly understood interprets a sacred text for the life of a community and its members. The interpretation may be direct and explicit or implicit, may begin with the text or begin with a situation, but some conversation between contemporary concerns and scripture is included in every sermon" (David L. Bartlett, Sermon, Concise Encyclopaedia of Preaching, p. 433). Here in lies the importance of a sermon. Three things are vitally important, scripture, community of the faith and interpretation in the context of worship. David Bartlett rightly describes the importance of the sermon by portraying the various functions of a sermon (Ibid, pp. 433-35).

1. Sermons may be *kerygma, proclamation* of what God has done in Jesus Christ and calling people for the decision of faith. See Acts 2.14-30, 3.12-26 and 1 Cor. 2.1-5.
2. Sermons may be *Didache, teaching*. Every sermon will include some instruction about the biblical text in its context and about the conduct of people in their covenant relationship with God.
3. Sermons may be *paraklesis, exhortation*. They are persuading for a godly life and comforting for troubled.
4. Sermons may be *anamnesis, remembrance*. "The purpose of sermons that function as anamnesis is to strengthen the congregations or believers sense of identity – defined, strengthened, and shaped by the memories embodied in text and tradition" Ibid, p. 434.

5. Sermons may be *makarism, blessing.* "The purpose of sermons whose function is blessing is to inspire gratitude and delight" Ibid. See Pgs. 103.1, Mt. 5.1-11, etc.
6. Sermons may be *Sophia, wisdom.* Sermons point to the orders and disorders in everyday life of the world and connect them to the shared values perceptions within the faithful community based on the scripture. See Proverbs, 1 Cor. 6.12, 8.1 etc.
7. Sermons may be *prophetic, prophecy.* "The purpose of such prophetic sermons is not primarily to induce guilt or to stir controversy but to place human responsibility within the framework of the divine commitment to justice and compassion. Often prophetic sermons move to a call to repentance and renewal, for the preacher and the congregation alike" Ibid, p. 435.
8. Sermons may be *parabole, parable.* Sermons may use metaphors or similies drawn from common life and show the uncommon dealings of God with humanity. See 2 Sam. 12-1-6, Luke 10.25-37, 15.11-32 etc.

"*Go into all the world and proclaim the good news to the whole creation.*" Mark 16.15

Bibliography

Bartlett, D. L. The Shape of Scriptural Authority, 1983.

Cleophus La Rue, The Heart of Black Preaching, 2000 and Power in the Pulpit, 2002.

Karl Barth, Homiletics, 1991.

Charles Bartow, God's Human Speech, 1997.

The New Interpreters Handbook of Preaching, 2008.

William Willimon and Richard Lischer, Concise Encyclopaedia of Preaching, 1995.

Richard Lischer, ed. The Company of Preachers, Wisdom on Preaching, Augustine to Present, 2002.

James D. Berkley, general editor, Leadership Handbooks of Practical Theology, vol. One, Word and Worship, 1992.

D. W. Cleverly Ford, The Ministry of the Word, 1979.

Michael Duduit, ed. Handbook of Contemporary Preaching, 1992.

Chapter 14

What is the Impact of Theological Education in the Life and Ministry of the Pastors and Preachers?

'To equip the saints for the work of ministry, for building up the body of Christ.'

Ephesians 4:12(NRSV)

Equipping the Church for the Work of Ministry. This is the basic point that is fundamental for the theological education enterprise. There is no dispute over the fact that theological education and ministerial formation has an impact on the life and work of the pastors and preachers.

Streams of Theological Education in India

I. Theological Training and Ministerial Formation in India

Theological Training and Ministerial Formation takes place through at least three major streams in India:

1. **The Catholic Bishops Conference in India** guides the training of the catholic priests. There are innumerable theological seminaries of the Catholic Church in India. In fact, it is a very lengthy process of training for priesthood,

three to four years of philosophical study in the first instance and then another four years of theological study and formation.

2. **The Senate of Serampore College in Kolkata,** with university rights, directs the theological training of most of the Protestant churches through its affiliated colleges and seminaries spread all over India. The Senate has a Board of Theological Education with representatives from the colleges and the churches in India. Besides giving affiliation to colleges and seminaries, the Senate runs two major programmes, namely the doctoral and research programmes through the South Asia Theological and Research Institute (SATHRI) and continuing education of the pastors; theological education for the lay people and other external courses (non-residential) through the Senate Centre for Extension and Pastoral Theological Research, (SCEPTRE).
3. **The Asian Theological Association,** formed some years ago, gives affiliation to some of the colleges and seminaries with an evangelical emphasis, which give training to students. Some of them do receive the certificates and degrees from the Senate of Serampore. There are also some colleges and institutions of private nature owned by individuals who contribute towards theological education.

II. Now Let us Look at the Church Situation in India

The church in India consists of all the major Christian traditions namely the Roman Catholic, the orthodox, the protestant and the charismatic. All of them together constitute about 3% of the total population. The overwhelming majority are the Hindus (81%), then Muslims (13%) and then others like Sikhs, Buddhists, etc. constitute the rest. This means the church in India exists amid a multi-religious, multilingual, and multicultural context.

Historical Perspectives

Traditionally it is believed that the Apostle Thomas came to India in the year 52 AD. And an empty tomb and a mountain 'St. Thomas Mount' where he is supposed to have been killed exist in Chennai as living symbols of this tradition along with a small community of St. Thomas Christians. According to this, Christianity came to India in the very first century. However, there are strong historical evidence of the existence of the church since the 4th century when the Syrian Christians came to India as refugees. Since then, this church exists in India as Orthodox Church with several variations – Syrian orthodox, Indian orthodox, the Jacobites, the Mar Thoma, Chaldean etc. – but all have the common emphasis on the rich liturgical tradition of the ancient church. Though the several orthodox churches carry on institutional mission through schools and colleges, their main expression of faith consists of the ancient liturgical traditions namely the Anaphora or the St. James liturgy.

The Roman Catholics came to India in the 16th century and continue to exist as the major wing of the Christianity with about 50% of the total Christians. Though very closely related to the church and papal authority in Rome, the Roman Catholic Church in India, since the Vatican II, has been trying to develop itself into an Indian church in its content and form. Many of the local traditions have been adopted in the worship and lifestyle of the Roman Catholic Christians. The ecclesiology is that of native perspective, though in the structure and organisation, the Roman Catholic Church continues to be just as the other Roman Catholic churches in other parts of the world. Its service in the society through education, healing, social service is unparalleled. The Roman Catholic Church has brought in a diaconal approach to Indian ecclesiology with its charitable services in the society; the notable among them is the sisters of charity founded by the Mother Theresa. Along with other churches the Roman Catholic Church has been emphasising the church's action to change the structures of society in the direction of justice. The protestant church traditions began to come to India at the beginning of the 18th century with the coming of Ziegenbalg from Leipzig. Ever since almost all the protestant missions worked in India and established their forms of Christianity. However, the ineffectiveness of the life and work of the divided church was realised in the beginning of the 20th century and several protestant churches began to negotiate seriously the Church Union. As a result of prayerful and careful union negotiations, and with a zeal to establish the Indian church, the Church of South India was formed in 1947 with the Episcopal and non-Episcopal traditions becoming a united Episcopal ecumenical church. Thus, the ecumenical church unity element of the church was brought into the Indian ecclesiology. Ever since the CSI has been a pioneer model in Church Union negotiations, whose effects resulted in the formation of the Church of North India, the uniting churches in Australia, the churches of Christ in USA and others in England.

Christianity as a religion or as a faith community is one according to the Indian Constitution, Indian Census, and Indian welfare schemes. But in reality, there are many churches based on, historical beginnings, different theological positions, faith interpretations, doctrines, order of worship services, ministry patterns and even lifestyle. There are as many different churches in India as there are in rest of the world. We might broadly classify them as:

The Roman Catholic, the Orthodox, the Ecumenical/united churches like the CSI and the CNI, the Lutheran, the Methodist, the Baptist, the Neo - Apostolic, the brethren, the Pentecostal, and other free churches.

The Church affiliations are also varied:

The Roman Catholic Church under the Catholic Bishops Conference in India.

The Orthodox churches are under the Orthodox umbrella.

The Lutheran under the Union of Evangelical Lutheran Churches in India.

Major Protestants under NCCI (30 Member Churches),

Free Churches under All India Council of Churches.

Evangelical Churches under the Evangelical Fellowship of India.

Purpose of Theological Education

Theological Institutions are the think tanks and reflective wings of the church. The primary task is to understand and interpret the scriptures and tradition/s of the church. That which has been handed down from ages is to be understood and interpreted meaningful in each age and generation.

Empowering the church in its faith and practice is the primary purpose of Theological Education. This empowerment takes place in and through the various ministries within the church. Worship, Christian preaching and teaching, Breaking of the Bread (commonly called Holy Communion, Eucharist, Lord's Supper etc), Prayer, and Christian Fellowship, Service and Witness - Leiturgia, Kerygma, Koinonia, Diakonia, Marturia - are the central activities of the church. (See Acts of the Apostles 2.42 - The Church i.e., the believers continued steadfastly in the apostles' doctrine and fellowship and in breaking of bread and in prayers. That is the Church). Here, has a pastor and preacher, a great responsibility.

1. Church exists for Mission and mission is Kerygma – proclamation of the Gospel – the Good News of Jesus Christ and the salvation that he has provided through his life, death and resurrection. The Church as the Body of Christ and as a community of the believers, in its life and work endeavours to bear witness to the Gospel wherever it is placed. Mission is not aggressive propaganda but a way of life. The local congregations need to be equipped to show the love of Jesus to the community around them. Individual members of the Church in their life and actions shall endeavour to bear witness to the Gospel wherever God has called them to be. Dialogue with the people of other faiths becomes an occasion for the church to share the Gospel as well as to learn from them. True mission is

carried out in a spirit of openness to and respect for other faiths, avoiding any attitude of triumphalism.

2. Church is to nurture the people of God through worship, preaching, Christian education and pastoral care, thus building up koinonia, deepening spirituality and empowering them to be fruitful instruments in mission. Through theological education the church seeks to equip its people for mission through interpreting its faith that is relevant to the contemporary world. The Church pays special attention to children and new believers in Christian nurture.
3. Church exists for Diakonia – service with dedication. As Christ served the people with love and compassion, the church seeks to engage itself in the service of the people. The Church believes that the service rendered through its medical and educational institutions, children's homes, rural development projects and other diaconal ministries are an essential part of the mission entrusted to it. The church extends its service to all people irrespective of caste or creed but with a preferential option for the poor and the neglected in the society.
4. Church is to strive to establish justice in society. The church seeks to establish a just, participatory, and reconciling society. This means to transform unjust structures, to denounce all forms of domination and exclusion and to work towards equal and participant patterns of relationships. It also means renewing cultures and working for peace and reconciliation. The church seeks to equip its members to actively participate in the building up of the nation through involvement in political structures and people's movements. This will also mean that the church needs to be prepared to work together with others whose aims and strategies are consonant with the values of the Kingdom.

5. Church is called to stewardship of God's creation. The church seeks to create awareness among its members about environmental and ecological concerns and thereby to care for God's creation. It endeavours to encourage its members to refrain from excessive exploitation of nature's resources and to strive to keep the earth a habitable place for the present as well as future generations.

Chapter 15

What are Some of the Methods for Bible Study?

The study of the Bible is one of the most important things in the faith and practice of the church. It enables the members of the church to understand the Bible. It also enables the church to hear God's word afresh and discern what is God saying today. God spoke and continues to speak through the testimony of the Holy Scriptures. The Bible study could be within a group or for individuals.

Fundamental Principles in Bible Study

I. The meaning of the passage in its original setting.
   What did the passage mean in its original context?
   a. What is the literary form of the text?
   b. What is the common sense/superficial meaning of the text in its first reading?
   c. What does the text mean in the light of the exegesis? Translation, textual problems etc.
   d. What is the historical and social setting of the passage? Historical situation of its writing, customs of the time,

circumstances that lead to its writing and the message of the time.

II. The meaning if the passage for us here and now.

What does it mean for us here and now?

a. In what way is our situation similar to that of the original readers?

b. What is God saying to me personally?

In my home, place of work and in the church?

c. What does it mean for the ministry of the church?

d. What is God saying to the world and our country?

III. Our response to God's message.

What can be our message to God's message?

The purpose of knowing the Bible is to respond to God in faith and in action.

Practical Suggestions for Bible Study

a. All should have the above guidelines.

b. All need to read the passage keeping in mind the guidelines.

c. With one leader all share their thoughts and responses.

d. Finally arrive at some concrete conclusions and actions.

Some common Methods of Bible Study

1. Iona Method: Developed in Scotland

a. Leader introduces the passage with the background.

b. A member reads the passage.

c. The whole group reads the passage silently.

d. Members share what they consider as important.

e. The leader sums up the discussion.

f. The group decides about an action programme.

2. Swedish Method: Developed in Sweden

Each person is given a paper on which a question mark, an arrow and a candle have been drawn. The group will be given 10 to 15 minutes to read and think and note down on the paper – questions they have, anything that has pricked their conscience, or a new insight against the markings.

a. The leader introduces the passage.
b. The passage is read aloud.
c. Members work on their own.
d. After a while all come together and share in discussion
e. The leader sums up by adding anything that needs to be said.
f. An action programme is planned by the group after the discussion.

3. Attungal Method: Developed in Kerala, India

a. The leader introduces the passage.
b. The passage is read aloud by a member.
c. The members are supplied with a piece of paper which is vertically divided, on the left is written about God and on the right about human beings.
d. The members read the passage silently and note down whatever they see as referring to God and human beings.
e. After some time when everyone is ready, general discussion will follow.
f. The leader sums up the discussion and a course of action is planned.

4. Inductive Method: Developed in the United States

a. The leader starts with a particular idea in the passage.
b. The members read the passage either with that idea or any other.
c. All share their specific concerns and move on the decide.

5. **Deductive Method: Developed in the United States**
   a. The leader starts with the general or main idea of the passage.
   b. All members read the passage with a view of making the general idea specific.
   c. All share their specific concerns and move on to decide.
6. **Reading the Bible through the Eyes of Another** (EMS, Stuttgart, Germany).
7. **Re-reading the Bible** (Dyan Chand Carr, Tamil Nadu Theological Seminary, Madurai, India).
8. **Hans-Ruedi Weber, Experiments with Bible Study,** WCC Publications, Geneva, 1981.

Chapter 16

Daily Devotions on Subhvartha TV Broadcast in 2015 to 2016

Shubhavartha TV - Morning Devotions: Reflections for Daily Living

Values of Life

TIME

1. Time is God´s gift, Psalm 118.24
2. Our time is in God´s hand, Psalm 31.15
3. Times and Seasons are set by God´s authority, Acts 1.7
4. Good and Bad Use of time, Ephesians 5.15
5. God measures our life (use of time), Daniel 5.26
6. Begin the Day with God, Mark 1.35
7. End the Day with God, Mark 1.32

WORK

8. Work is worship, Importance of Work, 2 Thessalonians 3. 6-15.
9. Satisfaction in Work, Isaiah 28.23-29; Ecclesiastes 2.17-26.

10. Testing the quality of work, 1 Corinthians 3.13
11. Equipped for every good work, 2 Timothy 3.17, Matthew 5.16
12. Do not destroy the work of God, Romans 14.20
13. Do the work of an evangelist, 2Timothy 4.5
14. Created in Christ Jesus for good works, Ephesians 2.10, Colossians 3.12-14

FRIENDSHIP

15. Importance of Friendship, Ecclesiastes 4.7-12
16. Faithfulness in Friendship, Proverbs 27.6,10,17
17. God spoke to Moses as with a friend, Exodus 33.11, God´s friendship
18. Friendship with the world is enmity with God, James 4.4
19. A true friend loves at all times, Proverbs 17.17, John 15.13
20. Example of friendship – David and Jonathan, 1 Samuel 20
21. Jesus calls the disciples friends, John 15.15

22-28. Family/Relationships

29-35. Goodness, Sacrifice

36-42. Kindness, Compassion

43-49. Sincerity

50-56. Honesty

57-63. Patience

64-70. Caring

71-77. Hospitality

78-84. Happy, Joy, Joyful, Laughter,

85-91. Comforting

92-98. Blessed, Blessing,

99-105. Conscience

106-112. Courage, Boldness, Fearlessness

113-119. Temptation, Ensnared
120-126. Self-Control
127-133. Forgiveness
134-140. Freedom
141-147. Gentleness
148-154. Grace
155-161. Guidance
162-168. Giving, Generosity
169-175. Health, Healing
176-182. Hypocrisy
183-189. Truth/Integrity
190-196. Judging others
197- 213. Life, Purpose of,
214-220. Love
221-227. Prosperity, Gold, Wealth, Money, Greed
228-234. Humility, Meekness
235-241. Obedience
242-248. Popularity
249-255. Wisdom
256-262. Peace, Quietness
263-269. Stewardship
270-276. Thankfulness
277-283. Anxiety, Discouragement, Distress
284-290. Hope, Assurance, Confidence
291-297. Ability
298-304. Abundance, Fullness
305-311. Responsibility/Accountability
312-318. Anger
319-325. Authority, Power

326-332. Beauty, Beautiful

333-339. Boasting, Pride

340-346. Devotions

347-353. Discipleship

356-362. Godliness

363-365. Holiness

Chapter 17

Know Your Bible

An Outline of a Seminar Conducted at the Church of St. John the Baptist in 2017 in Secunderabad

(Phoenician *Byblos* to Greek *Biblos* to English *Bible,* the *Book*)

1. How the Bible came to be the BIBLE?

   The Hebrew Scriptures – the Old Testament

      The Bible Jesus read, used and loved

      Why is it written in Hebrew?

      What constitutes OT?

      Why it is Old Testament?

      When it became authoritative scriptures?

      How is it related to the New Testament?

      How is it related to the Islamic Scriptures?

      Why some books are treated as apocryphal and rejected by the Protestant Churches?

2. The Christian Scriptures – the New Testament

   Why is it written in Greek?

   What constitutes the NT?

Why it is New Testament?

When it became authoritative scriptures?

How is it related to the Old Testament?

3. The Lost Books of the New Testament

   Why are some Gospels and Letters rejected and went into oblivion?

4. The Divine WORD in the human words

   How could the human language become divine Word?

5. The Bible in History and History in the Bible

   What is the Impact of the Bible in the World History?

   What is the World History Influence on the Bible?

6. The Bible and the Reformation

   Why the Bible became sole inspiration for the Reformation of the Church?

7. The Bible and Mission

   What is Missio Dei and how it is presented in the Bible?

8. The Bible and Ecumenism

   What is Ecumenism and how it is grounded in the Bible?

9. The Bible Today

   What is the status of the Bible in Church and Society?

10. The Bible and you and me and us

    What does it matter?

    How does it matter?

Chapter 18

The Bible Speaks Again

(Lenten Friday Thematic Devotions 2016
by the Rt. Rev. Dr. P. Surya Prakash, CSI Bishop Emeritus.

Wesley Church Clock Tower, Secunderabad
Medak Diocese, Church of South India).

12.02.2016 The Bible in History

19.02.2016 The Bible: Divine Word, Human Word

26.02 2016 The Bible and the Reformation

04.03.2016 The Bible and Mission

11.03.2016 The Bible and Ecumenism

18.03.2016 The Bible Today

The Bible Speaks and Let the Bible Speak Again

Preliminary Remarks

St. Pauls Missionary Journeys transformed the first century Mediterranean world, that is Europe today.

The Roman Emperor Constantine's conversion to Christianity in the 4th century AD evangelised Europe.

The Magna Carta 1215 (Charter of Liberties) of King John and the Archbishop paved the way for democracy in Europe, (An original copy is kept in Salisbury Cathedral, England, and the other copy in the British Museum, London).

The Reformation of 1517 in Germany brought in Church Reforms and church splits too.

The Roman Catholic and Protestant Churches.

Period of Enlightenment of the 17th and the 18th centuries created Christian Culture in Europe, which later spread to America and Australia.

The beginning of Christian Missions and Organisations in Europe in 16th and 17th centuries.

King Henry VIII decision in 1735 to declare himself independent of Rome, led to the separation of the British Church from the Roman Catholic Church, came to be known as Church of England.

Rev. John Wesley and Rev. Charles Wesley preaching led to the Great Revival in the Church of England and the birth of the Methodist Church.

Democracy: 1789 French Revolution paved the way for freedom and liberty in Europe.

Civil Rights Movement in U.S. led to the abolition of slave trade in 1862.

Human Rights Legislation 1948 of UNO, led to Women's Rights, Children's Rights and later protection of Ecology and Environment,

Liberation/Independence Movements in Asia, Africa and Latin America made independent nations of the former colonies like India, Indonesia etc.

The Bible Changes History and Transforms It

It is divine Word, 2 Timothy 3.16, inspired Word.

It is Gods Word, Gods Commandments, Psalm 119.

God speaks through his prophets, Thus says the Lord, Co Aamar Jahweh.

Gods human speech, human word, Hebrews 1.1.

St. John 6.68, words of eternal life.

The Gospel of Mathews–fulfilment of Gods Law and the Prophets.

The Gospel of Mark – Jesus, Son of God, Son of Man, Good News of the Gospel.

The Gospel of Luke – Orderly Account of the Jesus of Nazareth, Lord and Saviour.

The Gospel of John – that they may believe; that they may continue to believe.

The Acts of the Apostles - Gospel from Jerusalem to Rome.

St. Pauls Letters – Church, Theology, Faith, Life and Witness.

I. The Bible in History

The Bible is not a history book but there is History in the Bible.

Nations and Peoples in the Bible

Amalekites

Egyptians

Ammonites (Jordan)

Arabians

Aram

Asia

Assyrians

Babylonians

Canaanites

Chorazines

Cyprus

Persians

Greeks

Philistines

Syrians

Romans

Israelites

Judah/Jews

Empires in the Bible

3000 to 1000 B.C Egypt, The Book of Exodus

1600 to 1300 B.C. Hittites, The Book of Judges

1010 to 931 B.C. Israel, the Books of Samuel and Kings

900 to 612 B.C. Assyrians, The Book of 2 Kings

612 to 539 B.C. Babylonians, The Book of Daniel

549 to 331 B.C. Persians, The Book of Isaiah

600 to 300 B.C. Greeks, Inter-Testamental period (300 B.C. - A.D)

275 to 210 B.C. Romans, Apocryphal writings (Maccabees, Esra, Tobit etc.)

Gods Judgement on Israel's Neighbours:

Israel's neighbouring nations, Amos 1–2

Neighbouring nations are instruments in God's hands, Isaiah 44.28; 45.1.

God liberates other nations too. Amos 9.7–8.

II. The Bible: Divine Word, Human Word

The Law – Gods Will revealed, becomes Gods Word in the form of statutes and commandments.

The Prophets – God speaking through prophets becomes Gods Word.

The Writings – Job, Psalms, Proverbs, Ecclesiastes, Song of Solomon become Gods Word in the literary form of poetry.

The New Testament:

The Gospels – Word became flesh and dwelt among us full of grace and truth in Jesus Christ (Karl Barth, the Doctrine of the Word of God).

The Acts of the Apostles – the Proclaimer becomes the Proclaimed (Rudolf Bultmann, Christ proclaimed the Kingdom of God, Apostles proclaim Christ himself).

The Church proclaims Christ crucified, day after day, Sunday after Sunday, year after year.

The Bible Versions

The Bible Translations

The Bible Dictionaries

The Bible Commentaries

The Bible Word Studies

The Bible Sermon Helps

The Bible Daily Words

The Bible Expository Commentaries

God's Word in human words.

God's Word transforms human life and culture, e.g. North East India, Dalits in South India.

III: The Bible and the Reformation

October 31, 1517, Martin Luther nailed his 95 Theses on the Wittenberg Castle door, which are based on the Scriptures to bring about Reformation in the Catholic Church.

As a result, Reformation and eventually split in the Church.

The Context of Reformation

800–1500 called Dark Ages in Europe

Superstition, illiteracy, worship of saints and veneration of relics became the order of the day.

The Clergy became all powerful. Hierarchy of the Bishops and Priests became very authoritarian.

Power became corrupted.

The doctrines that took the centre stage:

a. Papacy – infallibility and all powerful, successor to St. Peter

b. Mariology – mediation of Mary, the mother of Jesus, and her veneration

c. Purgatory – the lamentation/tormentation of souls in fire in a place between heaven and earth called purgatory for purification. To get released one was required to buy Indulgences. Selling and buying of Indulgences became very common. Pope Leo X wanted to build the largest church, Basilica, which later came to be known as St. Peters Basilica in Rome. A priest by name Johann Tetzel was the papal fund-raiser, whose slogan was, when the coin rings in the box, the soul springs from the fire.

   In a way this became salvation by works, contrary to the Scriptures.

Martin Luther's Fundamental Theological Stance

Martin Luther was a priest and a professor of the New Testament at the Wittenberg Seminary. He was an Augustinian monk at the monastery too.

Sola Scriptura – Scripture Alone for the Authority

Sola Gratia – Grace Alone for the Salvation

Sola Fide – Faith Alone for Redemption

The Pope has no power over purgatory.

Luther was assisted by Melanchthon in Germany,

John Calvin in Geneva,

Ulrich Zwingli in Zurich and John Knox in Scotland.

The Bible was brought to the centre of worship.

Their followers, Martin Luther's became Lutherans, John Calvin and John Knox, Presbyterians and Ulrich Zwinglis, the Congregationalists.

Later in the 18th century, John Wesley, Charles Wesley and George Whitefield brought about the Great Revival in the Church of England. Their followers came to be known as the Methodists, as they followed a strict discipline of life especially morning, noon and evening devotions, reading of the Scriptures and Prayers etc.

1545 - 60 the Roam Catholic Church held the Council of Trent for Counter Reformation.

However, the Second Vatican Council held between 1963 and 1968 brought about many reforms and changes except in matters of Papacy, Celibacy, and Mariology.

However, the Catholics and the Protestants are closer than ever before, agreeing on many doctrines including, Baptism, Eucharist and Ministry, (BEM Document, Lima 1982).

However, the Catholic Church continue to give central authority to Scripture and Tradition and Papacy. Whereas the Protestants emphasize the Bible and the respective Constitutions.

The Bible is the Basis

Romans 5.1, 3.24, Galatians 2.16,

The Bible is central and supreme authority in matters of faith.

The Church Councils, determine right theology.

The Classical Creeds, affirm right faith statements and are absolute for the Ministry.

IV. The Bible and Mission

There is a denomination in A.P. called ***Bible Mission*** started by Mungamuri Devadass Ayyagaru.

Missio Dei, Mission of God, not of the Church but of God.

First and foremost is the proclamation of the Word of God. St. Mathews 28, St. Mark 16.

Social Action, St. Mathews 25

Diaconal Services, Acts 6

Life and Work Movement of 20th century.

Kinder Not Hilfe

Missio,

Misereor,

Bread for the World,

Caritas,

Christian Aid

and other International Development Church Agencies.

Educational Institutions – schools, colleges, training centres etc.

Healing Ministry – hospitals, dispensaries

Bible Translations after the Reformation resulted in many publications beginning with Gutenberg's, Luther Bible in German, whereby Reading and finding news ideas, people were inspired to share the Good News.

Isaiah 52.7 – Blessed are the feet of those who bring good news.

Isaiah 6.8 – Whom shall I send? And who will go? Here I am, send me.

The New Testament – Mathews 28. 19, Mark 13.10, 16.17 and Acts 1.8, 13.2-4, 47, and John 15.16, 17.18, 20-21

Other Texts

Romans 10.13-15, Mathews 24. 14, Luke 24.47, 49, Acts 26. 14 – 18, Revelation 14.6, Mathews 9.37, Luke 10.1-3, 17-19, 9.1, Mathews 10.1, Mark 6.7,

Christians began Forming Groups – later became Mission Societies, Mission Organisations, sent missionaries all over the world.

Mission Sending Missionaries

Movement: West to East and North to South.

India – Roman Catholics, Francis Xavier 1542.

Roman Catholic - Jesuits, Carmelites, Redemptors, Selacians, Franciscons, etc.

Protestants – Barthelomeo Ziegenbalg 1706, William Carey 1793 and others.

Anglican – Church Mission Society, Society for the Propagation of the Gospel now United Society Partners in the Gospel.

Lutheran – Leipzig Mission, Berlin Mission, United Evangelical Mission, etc. In Germany and Evangelical Lutheran Mission in America.

Baptist – Baptist Mission Society, Canadian Baptist Mission, American Baptist Mission.

Reformed – Basel Mission, London Mission Society (now Council for World Mission).

Methodist Mission Society, London and others.

The 18th and the 19th Centuries are Centuries of Missions

CSI – Methodist Mission in Hyderabad (Medak, Karimnagar), Mysore, Madras and Trichinopoly.

CMS/SPG Missions in Madras, Madhya Kerala, Tirunelvelli, Trichinoploy, Nandyal, Dornakal, and Krishna Godavary, East Kerala.

London Mission/North Arcot Mission – Vellore, Rayalaseema, Coimbatore, South Kerala, Kanya Kumari, Kollam.

Basel Mission – South Karnataka, North Karnataka, Coimbatore, North Kerala, Malabar.

North East India – Scottish Presbyterian and American Baptist Missions.

Other Missions

Mission to the Seafairers

Leprosy Mission

Medical Mission

Christopher Blinden Mission

Famous World Missionaries

Africa – David Livingstone of the LMS

India – William Carey of the BMS, Amy Carmichael

China – Hudson Taylor, Jonathan Goforth, Eric Liddel

Burma/Myamnar – Adoni Ram Judson of the BMS, US.

George Muller – a pioneer in establishing orphanages

Ecuador – Nate Saint and Jim Juliet

Famous Missionaries in India

Francis Xavier, Robert De Nobili, Mother Theresa – Roman Catholic

Henry Martin – Anglican

William Carey – Baptist

Stanley Jones – American Methodist

Alexander Duff - Presbyterian

Samuel Higgin Botham, Reformed

Joshua Marshman, Baptist

William Ward, Baptist

Barthelomeo Ziegenbalg, Lutheran

Isabella Kerr, Methodist

Sr. Joyce Woollard, Anglican

Ida Scudder – Reformed

Graham Staines - CMS Australia

Ferdinand Kittel, Hermann Gundert of the Basel Mission

Theological Colleges

Department of Mission Studies

Society of Indian Missiologists

Missions Academy, Hamburg

Centre for Mission Studies, Queens College, Birmingham

Overseas Missionary Study Centre, Ventnor and Princeton, New Jersey, US.

Centre for Mission Studies, Oxford, London

Publications

Stephen Neill, A Dictionary of World Missions

Distribution of the Bibles

19th century Gideons International started 1898 by John H. Nicholson and Samuel E. Hill, placing Bibles in Hotels and schools in Wisconsin.

British and Foreign Bible International in 1804 for production and distribution of Bibles.

1811, the establishment of the Bible Society of India.

Scripture Union 1868, started by Josiah Spiers for children in North Wales.

Daily Bible Readings 1879, started by Annie Mortsen of Keswick, England.

20th century Back to the Bible Movement in the United States.

The Southern States in U.S are called the Bible Belt.

1948 The beginning of the Billy Graham Evangelistic Crusades.

World Christianity

The Roman Catholics, 1.2 billions

The Eastern Orthodox, 0.5 millions

The Protestants, over 500 millions

The Independent/Pentecost/Charismatic, 0.5 million

What is Our Mission?

CSI Mission Statement Concise, Hope for Four Million

Mission Statement in the Constitution

(Proclamation, Worship, Fellowship, Diakonia, Witness)

VELCOM – Vision for Equipping Local Congregations for Mission

(Agape, Agenda, Analysis and Action)

Church with a Mission

India Missions

India Mission Society Tirunelveli

Bible Mission, Mungamuri Devadass, great lyric writer in Telugu, 12, 14, 440, 572 etc.

A Boat with the Cross is the symbol of Mission

V. The Bible and Ecumenism

Why Church is divided?

Why there are so many Traditions?

Why there are so many Denominations?

These are the questions we ask.

Major Divisions

The Eastern Orthodox

The Roman Catholics

The Major Protestants

The Pentecostal/Charismatic and other Independent Churches

What is that divides Roman Catholics and Protestants?

The Doctrine of Papacy

The Doctrine of Celibacy

The Role of Mary

The Understanding of the Canon, Eucharist etc.

The Canon – 66 books + Aphocryphal writings

The Eucharist – the real presence of Christ

What is that dividing the Protestant Churches?

a. Literal or spiritual interpretation of the Bible
b. Allegorical, analytical, analogical, cultural interpretations
c. Place of women in the churches
d. Baptism, its form and practice
e. Speaking in tongues
f. Organisation and administration of the Church (Church government)
g. Gifts of the Spirit
h. Predestination, miracles, millennium
i. Ordination of the clergy,
j. Role of the laity
k. Ownership
l. Power and Authority
m. Understanding of the Eucharist/Holy Communion

What can be done?

Distinguish between what is fundamental, undisputed truth and disputed points.

Fundamental – Gods Love, God's Grace

Secondary – Rituals, Practices and Methods

Pray for Enlightenment and Illumination.

See biblical reasons for new points

Try not to argue about different viewpoints

Let the Bible speak and let the Holy Spirit guide.

Biblical Basis for Unity

Psalm 133 – the blessedness of unity (priestly, sacramental, liturgical).

John 17.20 – 25 – Godly unity, theological unity, divine unity.

Ephesians 4.1-16 Unity in the Body of Christ.

Doctrinal Unity

Unity of the Spirit in the bond of peace.

One Body

One Spirit

One hope of the calling

One Lord

One Faith

One Baptism,

One God, Father of all.

Unity in Diversity

The beauty of God's Creation is its Diversity

Mission and Missions

Christian Missions began to work each according to its tradition. This led to conflict of interest geographically and as a result confusion.

Some of the missionaries began to meet and discuss the issue.

As a result, Mission Comity was reached, an understanding not to be in competition to each other around the middle of 19th century,

The whole country was divided among the different Mission Societies.

Only after Independence of India, there are multiple denominations and church traditions in one place or city due to migration in search of livelihood and jobs.

Milestones in Church Unity

1910 International Missionary Conference in Edinburgh, Scotland Focussed on,

World Evangelism,

Mission Understanding and

Unity in Mission.

Life and Work Movement advocated the social responsibility of the church to meet the needs of the people in the society. The earliest and chief proponent was Archbishop Nathan Soderblom of Uppsala of the Swedish Lutheran Church. The first Universal Christian Conference on Life and Work met at Stockholm, August 19–30, 1925. The second meeting was called World Conference on Church, Community and State, met at Oxford 19–26 July 1937. Subsequently became a Commission of the WCC in 1948.

Faith and Order Movement, started after 1910 to deal with matters of Faith and Order of the Church and its Unity. The first meeting was held in 1927 with 394 delegates from 108 churches in Lausanne, Switzerland. It became the Faith and Order Commission of the World Council of Churches in 1948. BEM Document of Lima 1982 has been its important achievement. It works/publications on Week of Prayer for Christian Unity, and the date of Easter in collaboration with the Roman Catholic Church. It is a theological movement.

International Missionary Council emerged from the World Missionary Conference held at Edinburgh in 1910 and was established in 1921.

Second Mission Conference, 1929 International Missionary Council in Jerusalem

Third Mission Conference, 1938 International Mission Conference at Madras Christian College, Tambaram, Madras, India.

Theme: Christian Gospel in a Non-Christian World.

It merged with the WCC at New Delhi Assembly in 1961 and became a Commission on Mission.

John R. Mott, Archbishop Nathan Södorblom are considered to be the chief architects of the Ecumenical Movement. He laid foundation stone for UTC Bengaluru in November 1912.

Formation of the World Council of Churches in 1948 in Amsterdam, Holland

Head Quarters in Geneva, Switzerland

Ecumenical Institute Bossey, Geneva

General Assemblies of WCC

1st Assembly in Amsterdam, 22nd August to 4th September 1948,

Theme: Mans Disorder, Gods Design (147 churches)

2nd Assembly, Evanston, Illinois US, 5-31 August 1954

Theme: Christ – the Hope of the World (161 churches)

3rd Assembly, New Delhi, India 19 – 5 December 1961,

Theme: Jesus Christ – the Light of the World (197 churches)

Merger of IMC and joining of the Eastern Orthodox Churches

Focussed on Unity, Mission and Service

4th Assembly, Uppsala, Sweden, 4 – 20 July 1968,

Theme: Behold, I make all things new (churches 235)

Focussed on Social Gospel, The Roman Catholic observers participated

5th Assembly Nairobi, Kenya, 23rd November to 10th December 1975,

Theme: Jesus Christ Frees and Unites (churches 285)

Initiating the process of dialogue with other faiths and religions.

6th Assembly, Vancouver, Canada, 24 July to 10 August 1983,

Theme: Jesus Christ – the Life of the World (churches 301)

Focussed on Baptism, Eucharist and Ministry (Lima Document), Justice, Peace and Integrity of Creation

7th Assembly, Canberra, Australia, 7 – 20 February 1991,

Theme: Come, Holy Spirit. Renew the Whole Creation (churches 317)

Focussed on the Holy Spirit

8th Assembly, Harare, Zimbabwe, 3 – 4 December 1998,

Theme: Turn to God - Rejoice in Hope (churches 339)

Focussed on, Forum on Christian churches and ecumenical organisations

9th Assembly, Porto Alegre, Brazil, 14th to 23rd February 2006,

Theme: God, in your grace, transform the World (churches 348)

Focussed on called to be One Church.

10th. Assembly, Busan, Republic of South Korea, 30 October to 8th November 2013,

Theme: God of life, lead us to justice and peace (churches 345).

11th Assembly has been held in Karlsruhe, Germany 2021,

Current membership 325 churches

Parallel Evangelical Council – Lausanne Conference, started under the leadership of Dr. Billy Graham.

National Councils

National Council of Churches in India established 1913.

Regional Councils

Christian Council of Asia

Other Ecumenical Bodies:

EATWORT – Ecumenical Association of Third World Theologians

ECC – Ecumenical Christian Centre, Whitefield, Bengaluru

FOIM – Fellowship of Indian Missiologists

SBS – Society for Biblical Studies

CHAI – Church History Association of India

ISPCK – Indian Society for the Propagation of the Gospel

ICSA – Inter Church Social Action

CASA – Church Auxiliary for Social Action

BSI – Bible Society of India

YMCA/YWCA – Young Men/Women Christian Association

Various Commissions for Unity:

Roman Catholic Church with the Anglicans,

the Lutherans, the Reformed, the Orthodox, the Charismatic etc.

So also, Church of England.

Church Unity in India

1919 Tranquebar Conference of Indian leaders, called for unity by the Bishop V. S. Azariah of Dornakal, considered to be the chief architect of church unity in India.

1923 Joint Council was established to begin negotiations among the Anglicans, the Methodists, the Reformed.

Basis

Lambeth Quadrilateral: The Episcopacy, the Classical Creeds, the Old and New Testaments and the two Sacraments of Baptism and the Eucharist.

Issues

The Episcopacy

The Parity of Ministry

The Indian Church

The Conditions of Unity

The Governing Principles of the Church

The Basis of Union: The Scheme of Union

First edition 1927

Seventh edition 1941

Acceptance by the Methodists in 1943

by the Anglicans in 1945

by the South India United Church in 1944

They had to wait till the end of World War II

War ended in 1945 and India became independent in August 1947.

Immediately thereafter the united Church of South India was inaugurated on 27th of September 1947, at Georges Cathedral, Chennai.

It was acclaimed as the Second Pentecost, Ecumenical Wonder since the Episcopal and the Non-Episcopal Churches came together and formed an Episcopal Church after the Reformation.

Church of South India became a unique church in India.

Perhaps the first Organic Union of Churches after the Reformation.

Vision and Venture.

The very first Synod of the church in 1948 at Madurai called for unity of the churches in India,

The Lutheran churches responded positively, and negotiations were held till 1969. Even after agreeing to a new constitution and the name, the Church of Christ in South India, the Lutherans backed out just before inauguration.

Coimbatore Diocese joined CSI in 1950.

Basel Mission Churches joined the CSI in 1958 and 1968.

Nandyal Diocese joined the CSI in 1975.

Some churches of the SIUC in Ananthapur, and some other churches of the Basel Mission in Mangalore and Mumbai did not join the CSI.

However, church unity became a reality in North India in 1970 due to some influence of the church unity in the South. The new church is called the Church of North India.

The CSI and CNI together with the Mar Thoma Church formed a Joint Council in 1976.

It became a Communion of Churches in India in 2002.

A full pledged Constitution of CSI came about in 1952.

The three major traditions that came into the union were incorporated, namely the Moderator of the Reformed, the Diocesan Bishops, Presbyters and deacons of the Anglicans, and the Group or District chairman/woman of the Methodists

All other titles like Archbishop, Archdeacon, Vicar, Canon, Priest, Curate etc. were given up. Provinces and Parishes are replaced by Dioceses and Pastorates.

A complete book on worship prepared by the Liturgy Committee of the united church was published in 1962, called the CSI Book of Common Worship, revised extensively in 2002.

The Anglican worship book is called Book of Common Prayer, original 1662 and revised subsequently many times.

VI. The Bible Today

The process of how the Bible came to us.

First, the Papyrus sheets (the pulp from reeds in the river Nile, 1 – 2 centuries)

Second, the Parchment scrolls (animal skins, 1 – 2 centuries)

Later, the Printed pages (on paper, 16th century)

We are a privileged generation to have the Bible in the language we could read and understand.

The Bible is in our language

The Bible of our choice

Many choices in English – KJV, NIV, RV, RSV, NRSV, ESV, GNB, etc. (See also at the end).

The Bible with commentary

The Bible in bi-lingual, English and Telugu, Hebrew and English, Greek and English

The Bible with concordances, word studies, alternate texts (variations from manuscripts) Bibles

Digital Bibles

The One Year (1 to 5 chapters daily).

Translations

By 2000, in 6500 languages

337 complete Bible

799 only New Testament

4466 yet to have a Bible in their language

Translations from Hebrew and Greek to English

In 1812, translation of Telugu Bible, 1818 publication

Publications

Editions

Dictionaries

Commentaries

Word Studies

Concordances

The Bible Outlines by the Rev. C.W. Posnett

founded the theological college, he named it, Sathya Vedha Patashala in Medak

Archaeological Discoveries

Dead Sea Scrolls in 1948, brought new insights in the study and interpretation of the biblical texts.

The Bible and Art, Michel Angelo, Sistine Chapel Rome, stained glass windows with Nativity, Crucifixion and Resurrection scenes, Apostles and other Saints), Church on Mount Tabor with Jesus, Moses and Elijah, Church on Mount Carmel with Elijah,

Medak Cathedral: the Ascension Window 1927, the Crucifixion Window 1847 and the Nativity (birth of Christ) Window 1958 by the Artist Frank Salisbury.

The Bible and Music, Handels Messiah (the Alleluia Chorus), Mathews Passion of Johannes Sebastian Bach and others.

The Bible and Literature, John Milton, Paradise Lost, Paradise Regained, Gurram Joshuas, Christu Charitra, in Telugu,

The Bible and Films, Cecil de Mellows, King of Kings, Ten Commandments, the Greatest Story Ever Told, Ben Hur; Mel Gibson's, The Passion of Christ, Jaya Chanders, Karuna Mayudu in Telugu in India in 1978. and other.

The Bible and Hymns and Songs, Charles Wesley, Isaac Watts and others,

In Telugu, Purushotham Chaudary, Pulipaka Jagannatham, Mungamuri Devadass, A.B. Masilamony and others

The Bible and Spirituality, Micah 6.8

do justice

love kindness

and walk humble with your God.

K. C. Abraham´s interpretation: Passion for Justice, Compassion for People, Communion with God.

The Bible and Prayer, pray without ceasing, the biblical exhortation.

The Bible and Creeds, the Apostles Creed and the Nicene Creed

The Bible and Ordination, Minister of the Word.

The Bible and Liturgy, Praise and Thanksgiving, Minister for the Word and Sacrament,

The Bible and Revival,

The Bible and Evangelism, D. T. Niles, one beggar telling the other beggar where food is available.

The Bible and Ministry, teaching, preaching and healing

The Bible and the Sacraments, minister of the Sacraments

The Bible and Preaching, the Gospels are the narrative descriptions of the Apostolic preaching.

The Bible and St. Paul, Preaching of the Cross.

The Bible and Feminism, Women Empowerment, Equality

The Bible and Electronic Age, Cassettes, disks, Cds, videos, microchips, Usb etc.

The Bible and Daily Readings, Moravian Texts, Streams in the Desert, Upper Room, International Bible Readings Association,

The Bible and Daily Living

Lamp unto my feet and light unto my path, Psalm 119.105

I have kept your word in my heart, Psalm 119.11

Human Beings shall not live by bread alone, Luke 4.4

To whom shall we go, you have the words of eternal life, John 6.68

Psalm 1, 1

Bibliography

Bruce, F. F, and Others, **The Origin of the Bible**, published by GS Books, Hyderabad, 2015.

Mcquilkin, Robertson, **Understanding and Applying the Bible**, Moody Publishers, Chicago, 1983.

Water, Mark, **The Bible Made Plain & Simple**, OM publishing, Copy Right, 1999.

Achtemeier, Paul J, General Editor, **Bible Dictionary**, Theological Publications in India, Bengaluru, 2013.

Muthunayagam, Daniel Jones, **Bible Speaks Today**, Essays in Honour of Gnana Robinson, published by UTC, Bengaluru, 2000.

The Bible Speaks Again, A Guide from Holland, commissioned by the Netherlands Reformed Church, Augsburg Publishing House, SCM Press, 1969.

Readers Digest, **Atlas of the Bible**, An Illustrated Guide to the Holy Land, 1981.

The Oxford Companion to the Bible, edited by Bruce M. Metzger, Michael D. Coogan, Oxford University Press, 1993.

Dictionary of Biblical Imagery, an Encyclopedic Exploration of the Images, Symbols, Motifs, Metaphors, Figures of Speech

and Literary Patterns of the Bible, General Editors, Leland Ryken and James C. Wilhoit, Tremper Longman III, InterVersity Press, 1991

The Bible in Focus, ***A Pictorial of People, Places and Prophesies,*** compiled by Clem Clack, The Bible Society of Australia, 1987

Han Renckens, S.J. **A Bible of Your Own, Growing with the Scriptures,** Orbis Books, 1995, Priesthood of all Believers – not just clergy alone.

The Bible in English in English Translation, An Essential Guide, by Steven M. Sheeley and Robert N. Nash, Jr. Abingdon Press, Nashville 1997. Revised June/July 2020.

The Early Bible Translations

The Septuagint: Hebrew and Aramaic to Greek in about 300 BCE. It was intended for the Jews in Diaspora and took nearly two hundred years to translate by seventy scholars. NT writers used this Greek translation as their Bible.

The Vulgate: The entire Bible was translated into Latin from the original language by St. Jerome from Italy in Bethlehem. Later this Common Bible (Vulgar-Common) which became known as Vulgate, was the official Bible for over one thousand years.

Later appeared **Syriac, Coptic**, and other Versions.

The Bible English Versions

Early English Translations

The Coverdale Bible, 1535 by Myles Coverdale, translated from Vulgate and Martin Luther German Bible became official Bible, commissioned by the King Henry VIII.

Mathews Bible, 1537 by John Rogers using the pseudonym of Thomas Mathew, using Coverdales transaltion plus untranslated OT books by Tyndale.

The Great Bible, 1539 by Myles Coverdales revision of Mathews Bible, officially commissioned by Thomas Cranmer, the Archbishop of Canterbury used all over the Church of England.

The Geneva Bible, 1560, and the Bishops Bible 1568, translated by William Whittingham with Protestant leanings.

The Douay-Rheims Bible 1609, an English Catholic translation in France became the official translation for the Catholics till about 1940.

The King James Bible, 1611, by 54 renowned translators from the Universities of Oxford, Cambridge and Westminster, who divided themselves into six teams and exchanged translation of different parts of the Bible. It was officially authorised by King James I and thus became the Authorised Version for at least 300 years. It is one of the outstanding master pieces of English language then.

The Revised Version, 1885 in England, 1901 in United States and came to be known as the American Standard Version.

Major Translations

New International Version (NIV), 1973, verbal equivalence popular among the Evangelicals.

New American Standard Bible (NASB), 1971.

Living Bible, 1971, Easy translation of KJV.

King James Version (KJV), 1611.

New King James Version (NKJV), 1979, basically KJV with some modern words.

New English Bible with Apocrypha, 1970, Dynamic Equivalence, Oxford.

Revised English Bible, 1989, revision of NEB and REB.

J. B. – by J. B. Philips, NT in modern English, 1958 (dynamic equivalence) became popular among young people.

Revised Standard Version, NT 1946 and OT 1952 (verbal equivalence and excellent translation for study and worship.

Jerusalem Bible,1966, translated from French, good literary quality

New Jerusalem Bible, 1985, attempt to use inclusive language.

New Revised Standard Version, 1989, verbal equivalence, inclusive language.

The One Year Bible, arranged in 365 Daily Readings, 1991.

New American Bible, 1970, American Roman Catholic Edition.

New Living Translation, 1996, conservative evangelical version.

New American Standard Bible, 1995.

1976, dynamic equivalence.

Good News for Modern Man, Todays English Version, 1976, dynamic equivalence.

The Contemorary English Version, 1995, dynamic equivalence with emphasis on sound of the text.

International Childrens Bible, New Century Version, 1983.

The Amplified Bible, 1987.

Application Study Bible,1996, New Living Translation.

The New Interpreters Study Bible, 2003, NRSV with Apocrypha

The New Oxford Annotated Bible, 1991 NRSV with Apocryphal and Deuterocanonical Books.

The Wesley Study Bible, 2009, NRSV

English Standard Version, 2001 and is based upon the 1971 Revised Standard Version.

Translation Clusters

King James Version, Original 1611

Life Application Bible

Full Life Study Bible (Life in the Spirit Study Bible) 1992

Rainbow Children's Bible

The Original African Heritage Bible

The One Year Bible

New King James Version

The Young Explorers Bible
Life Application Bible for Students
Precious Moments Bible
Spirit Filled-Life Study Bible
Word in Life Bible

New International Version

Men's Devotional Bible
Women's Devotional Bible
NIV Study Bible
NIV Student Bible
New Adventure Bible for Kids

Attachment I

Additional Bibliography on Homiletics

The New Interpreters Handbook of Preaching, Abingdon Press, Nashville, 2008.

The Company of Preachers, *Wisdom on Preaching, Augustine to the Present,* Richard Lischer, Editor, William B. Eerdman Publishing Company, 2002.

Leadership Handbooks of Practical Theology, Volume One, *Word and Worship,* General Editor, James D. Berkley, Baker Book House, Grand Rapids, Michigan, 1992.

Handbook of Contemporary Preaching, Michael Duduit, Editor, Broadman & Holman Publishers, 1992.

Concise Encyclopaedia of Preaching, William H. Willimon & Richard Lischer, editors, Westminster John Knox Press, 1995.

D. W. Cleverley Ford, The Ministry of the Word, *the Preacher Must Preach to the Church in Order that the Church may preach to the world,* Hodder and Stoughton, 1978.

C. Barnabas. *Introduction To Homiletics,* Tiruchy, Indian Institute of Missiology, 2001.

John S. Sahayam. *Homiletics. Bangalore: Centre for Contemporary Christianity,* 2010.

Bartow, Charles L. *Preaching Moment: A Guide To Sermon Delivery.* Nashville, Abingdon, 1980.

Buttrick, David. *Homiletic: Moves and Structures.* Philadelphia, Fortress Press, 1987.

Jones, D. Martyn Lloyd. *Preaching & Preachers.* Grand Rapids, Zondervan Publishing House, 1971.

Lloyd - Jones, D. Martyn. *Preaching And Preachers.* Hodder and Stoughton Publishers, 1985.

Stott, John. *I Believe in Preaching.* London, Hodder & Stoughton, 1983.

Stott, J. R. W. *The Preacher's Portrait.* London, Tyndale Press, 1961.

Stott, John. *I Believe in Preaching.* London, Hodder & Stoughton, 1986.

Stott, John. *The Preacher's Portrait: Great Word Pictures from The New Testament (Christian Classic Series).* England, InterVarsity Press, 1996.

Stuempfle, Jr. Herman G., *Preaching Law and Gospel,* Fortress Press, Philadelphia, 1978.

English, Donald., *An Evangelical Theology of Preaching,* Abingdon Press, Nashville, 1996.

Burrell, Maurice., *Preparing to Preach, A Handbook for Preachers,* Athena Press, London, 2005.

Weber, Hans-Ruedi., *Jesus and the Children, Biblical Resources for Study and Preaching,* WCC, Geneva, 1979.

Troeger, Thomas H., *Ten Strategies for Preaching in a Multimedia Culture,* Abingdon Press, Nashville, 1996.

Sangster, E. William, *The Craft of Sermon Illustration,* Prickering and Inglis Glasgow, reprinted 1980.

Mathewson,D. Steven, *The Art of Preaching Old Testament Narrative,* Baker Academic, 2002.

Norrington, C. David, T*o Preach or Not to Preach?* Paternoster, 1996.

Gunton, E. Colin, *Theology Through Preaching,* T&T Clark, 2001.

Robinson, W. Haddon, *Expository Preaching, Principles and Practice,* InterVarsity Press, 1991.

The Canterbury Preachers Companion 2006 edited by Dr. J. Critchlow, The Canterbury Press.

Mitchell, P. Jolyon, *Visually Speaking, Radio and Renaissance of Preaching,* T&T Clark, Edinburgh, 1999.

Theology of Preaching, *Essays on Vision and Mission in the Pulpit,* edited by Gregory Heille, 2001.

Loscalzo, A. Craig, *Preaching Sermons that Connect,* InterVarsity Press, 1992.

Taylor B. John, *Preaching Through the Prophets*, Mowbray, London, 1983.

Gowan, E. Donald, *Reclaiming the Old Testament for the Christian Pulpit*, T&T Clark, Edinburgh, 1981.

Thielicke, Helmut, T*he Waiting Father, Sermons on the Parables of Jesus,* translated with an introduction by John W. Doberstein, James Clarke, London, 1959.

Thielicke, Helmut, *Christ and the Meaning of Life, Sermons and Meditations,* James Clarke and Co. 1965.

Theissen, Gerd, *Signs of Life, Sermons, and Meditations*, SCM Press 1991.

Sangster, E. William, *The Craft of Sermon Construction*, Pickering and Inglis, 1978.

Gilmore, Alec, *Preaching as Theatre*, SCM Press, 1991.

Labberton, Mark, *The Dangerous Act of Loving Your Neighbour,* Seeing *Others through the Eyes of Jesus,* IVP Books, 2010.

Brueggemann, Walter, *Inscribing the Text, Sermons and Prayers,* Fortress Press, 2004.

Brueggemann, Walter, *The Threat of Life, Sermons on Pain, Power and Weakness,* Fortress Press, 1996.

Porter E. Stanley, *Hearing the Old Testament in the New Testament,* William B. Eerdman Publishing Company, 2006.

Greidanus, Sidney, *The Modern Preacher and the Ancient Text,* William B. Eerdman Publishing Company, 1988.

Kalas, J. Ellsworth, *Preaching in an Age of Distraction,* 2014.

5,000 Quotations for Teachers and Preachers, compiled by Robert Backhouse, Kingsway Publications, 1994.

Griffiths, Michael, *Take My Life*, Authentic, 1967.

Campbell, Roger, *Preach for Year, 104 Sermon Outlines,* Authentic, 2014.

Wommack, Andrew, *Sharper than a Two-Edged Sword,* Vasanth Prints, Chennai, 1987.

Chandra Kumar, M, *Which Way Lord?* Authentic, 2007.

Gibson, M. Scott, *Preaching for Special Services,* Authentic, 2007.

Narrative Reading, *Narrative Preaching,* edited by Joel B. Green and Michael Pasquarelli III, Baker Academic, 2004.

Hans-Ruedi Weber, *Experiments with Bible Study,* WCC Publications, Geneva 1981.

Attachment II

Basic Course on Homiletics

Course Description

The author has taught the course for several years at the International College of Cultural Studies of the Good Shepherd Church (formerly the Operation Mobilization of India) for M.Div. students. The author acknowledges and thanks the International College of Cultural Studies of the Good Shepherd Church.

This course deals with the art and science of biblical preaching so that the people of God would be equipped and strengthened in their walk with God. The course does not presume to do everything in the field of preaching using all different means of modern communication theories. However, the course does sharply focus awareness of the key issues in the preaching ministry today. The course includes the life of the preacher, the text, and the sermon preparation and finally the actual sermon.

Course Objectives

1. This course aims at helping students realize that biblical preaching will change lives.
2. The students may realize the importance of biblical preaching.

3. Prepare the students with the principles and skills of sermon preparation and delivery.
4. Inspire and motivate the students to get involved in preaching ministry.
5. It seeks to identify the pressing current issues and to chart a reasonable and prudent course for the students.

Course Outcomes - Expectations

1. Know the principles and methods of preparing a sermon.
2. Having preached and evaluated, the students know to deliver a sermon.
3. The life of the student changes and will bring changes in the life of the congregation.
4. Know the needs of the congregation and prepare sermons accordingly.
5. Will regularly get involved in the ministry of preaching.

Course Outline

1. The Preacher

   The Preparation of the Preacher

   God's Call of the Preacher

   God's Anointing of the Preacher

   God's Enlightenment of the Preacher

   The Attitude Ingredient of the Preacher

   The Disciplines of the Preacher

   The Preacher's Library

   The Preacher's Desk

   The Preacher's Altar

   The Preacher's Listening Ear

2. The Sermon

   Preaching Themes: Search and Nurture

The Primary Secret of Finding Themes
Characteristic Development of Sermon
Planning Guide of a Sermon
Preaching Storehouse of a Preacher
The Marks of a Good Introduction
Why Introductions are important?
How Introductions impact the Preaching?
General Hints for Producing Introductions
When to Write the Introduction
Shaping the Body of the Sermon:
Steps to Body Building
Sermon Making as Art
Putting It All Together
The Making of Conclusion
Ways to Conclude
Some mistakes to Avoid.
Some Tips to Remember
The Principle of Illustrations/Pictures
Biblical Preaching Employs the Pictures/Illustrations
Some Commonalities of Pictorial Language
The Dangers of Picture/Illustrations
Asking Some Key Questions
Types of Sermons
Textual Sermon
Expository Sermons
Topical/Thematic Sermons
Biographical Sermons
Narrative Sermons
Lectionary Preaching

3. The Preaching/Delivery
   The Basis of Pulpit Communication
   The Genius of Communication
   The Techniques of Pulpit Communication
   Putting It All into Perspective
   The Preparation before Delivery
   Work as If It All Depends on You
   Pray as If It All Depends on God
   General Hints for Preparation

Core Textbooks

C. Barnabas. *Introduction To Homiletics.* Trichy, Indian Institute of Missiology, 2001.

John S. Sahayam. *Homiletics*. Bangalore: Centre for Contemporary Christianity, 2010.

Course Basics

1. Recognizing the importance of preaching ministry of the word
2. Learning the basic types of sermons and their significance.
3. Accepting the purpose of illustration in the sermon and what are the guidelines for a good illustration.
4. Acknowledging the terms Text and context in relation to preaching a sermon.
5. Knowing the qualities of a preacher.
6. Necessity of the basic steps one should follow in the preparation of the sermon.

Bibliography

Achtemeier, Elizabeth. *Preaching Hard Texts of The Old Testament.* Peabody, Hendrickson Publishers, Inc., 1998.

Adams, Jay E. *Preaching to the Heart: A Heart-to-Heart Discussion with Preachers of the Word.* Pittsburg, Presbyterian, and Reformed Publishing Co., 1983.

Studies In Preaching: Sense Appeal in The Sermons of Charles Haddon Spurgeon. Michigan, Baker Book House, 1976.

Barnabas, C. *Introduction to Homiletics.* Trichy, Indian Institute of Missiology, 2001.

Bartow, Charles L. *Preaching Moment: A Guide to Sermon Delivery.* Nashville, Abingdon, 1980.

Braga, James. *How To Prepare Bible Messages* (revised edition). Secunderabad, OM Books, 2003.

Buttrick, David. *Homiletic: Moves and Structures.* Philadelphia, Fortress Press, 1987.

Demaray, Donald E. *An Introduction To Homiletics.* Michigan, Baker Book House, 1978.

Grant, Reg, *The Power Sermon: Countdown to Quality Messages For Maximum Impact.* Grand Rapids, Baker Book House, 1993.

Hamilton, Donald L. *Homiletical Handbook.* Nashville, Broadman & Holman Publishers, 1992.

Jacks, G. Robert. *Getting The Word Across.* Grand Rapids, Wm.B. Eerdmans Publishing Co, 1995.

Jones, D. Martyn Lloyd. *Preaching & Preachers.* Grand Rapids, Zondervan Publishing House, 1971.

Kurian, Alexander. *Basic Homiletics and Expository Preaching: A Study Guide. Cooke Town,* Assembly Growth Ministries, 1995.

Lewis, Ralph L. *Inductive Preaching: Helping People Listen.* Illinois, A Division of Good News Pub. Croos Way, 1983.

Lloyd - Jones, D. Martyn. *Preaching and Preachers.* Hodder And Stoughton Publishers, 1985.

Macarthur, John. *Rediscovering Expository Preaching: Balancing the Science and Art of Biblical Exposition.* Pune, Grace to India, 1998.

Mcdill, Wayne. Twelve Essential Skills for Great Preaching. The, Broadman and Holman Publishers, 1996.

Perry, Lloyd M. *Biblical Preaching for Today's World.* Chicago, Moody Press, 1981.

Speaking To Life's Problems. Chicago, Moody Press, 1983.

Motyer, J. A. Expository Preaching Principles & Practice. InterVarsity Press, 1989.

Robinson, Haddon W. *Biblical Preaching: The Development and Delivery of Expository Messages.* Michigan, Baker Book House, 1980.

Spurgeon, C. H. *Eccentric Preachers. London,* Pass More & Alabaster, 1897.

Stewart, James E. *Heralds of God.* Baker Book House, 1972.

Stott, John. *I Believe in Preaching.* London, Hodder & Stoughton, 1983.

Stott, J. R. W. *The Preacher's Portrait.* London, Tyndale Press, 1961.

Stott, John. *I Believe in Preaching.* London, Hodder & Stoughton, 1986.

Stott, John. *The Preacher's Portrait: Great Word Pictures from the New Testament* (Christian Classic Series). England, Inter Varsity Press, 1996.

Vines, Jerry. *A Practical Guide to Sermon Preparation.* Chicago, Moody Press, 1985.

Wenger, E. Leslie. *Towards Maturity in Christ: A Study In Systematic Preaching* (The Christian Students' Library No: 38). Madras, The Christian Literature Society, 1966.

Wiersbe, Warren and David. *The Elements of Preaching,* Illinois, Tyndale House, 1986.

Wood, Beulah, *Turn the Key to Creativity: And Preach More Effectively,* Bangalore, SAIACS Press, 2003.

Attachment III

Theology of Worship and Sacraments

The author has taught the course for several years at the International College of Cultural Studies of the Good Shepherd Church (formerly the Operation Mobilization of India) for M.Div. students. The author acknowledges and thanks the International College of Cultural Studies of the Good Shepherd Church.

I. Course Description

This course is intended to equip students with essential and functional knowledge of the subject, through providing the Biblical, theological and historical foundations for worship, training skills for developing and leading congregational singing and teaching principles in planning worship services. This course also will cover the worship renewal of the 21st century and the current trends. It will also look at the practice of the sacraments as part of the worship.

II. Course Objectives

1. To feature the major themes and theological perspectives regarding worship with special emphasis on the importance of knowing God and His characteristics.

2. To trace the historical practices of worship and sacraments those are found in the church history.
3. To expose to the various forms of worship and practices those are followed in different churches and denominations.
4. To give an opportunity to each student to analyze, critique and evaluate practices of worship in today's context in the light of biblical teaching.
5. To developing a practical skill to plan and lead worship that is God-centered, biblically rooted, and realistic in nature.

III. Course Outcomes

1. Students understand the subject from biblical, cultural, and contemporary church practices.
2. Helps each student to understand the basics of worship and sacraments for all of life and ministry.
3. Students know to observe and analyze their own local church to reflect and to evaluate those practices in the light of biblical pattern.
4. Students will become the better worshipers of the Lord Jesus Christ personally through reflecting on spiritual discipline.
5. Prepared to influence the community/congregation with meaningful spiritual exercise.

IV. Course Outline

1. The Foundations of the study of Christian Worship
   1.1. Biblical Foundations
   1.2. Worship in the Old Testament (altar, tent, tabernacle, temple, festivals and fasting)
   1.3. Worship in the New Testament (individual, corporate, house church, prayer and fasting)
2. Historical Foundations
   2.1. Worship in the Early Church
   2.2. Developments during Ancient & Medieval period

   2.3. Worship during the Contemporary era including Pentecostal and Charismatic movements.

3. Theological Foundation of Christian Worship
   3.1. Nature of Christian Worship
      3.1.1. Response to Revelation
      3.1.2. Community Character of Worship
      3.1.3. Expression of faith
   3.2. Elements of Christian Worship: Meaning and significance of the following:
      3.2.1. Adoration
      3.2.2. Praise
      3.2.3. Confession
      3.2.4. Thanksgiving
      3.2.5. Intercession
4. Place of signs and symbols in worship

   Imagery in Worship: Cross, candles, choir, architecture of the church, bells, alter, pulpit and communion.
5. Forms of Worship

   Invocation, Litany, Psalm, Collect, Absolution, Reading of the Scripture, Sharing of Testimony, Offering, etc...
6. Liturgies
   6.1. The Bible as Liturgical Book: The Lectionary and Psalter
   6.2. Liturgy as Remembrance: The Christian Week and Year (Sacrifice, Communion)
   6.3. Structure of developed forms of Eucharistic liturgies (Liturgy of the word and sacrament in liturgical traditions)
   6.4. An evaluation of advantages and disadvantages of liturgies.
7. Non-Liturgical Worship

8. Contemporary Challenges to Christian Worship
    8.1. The Language of Worship
    8.2. Content, Structure and Style
    8.3. Indigenization of Worship
    8.4. Major efforts in the Roman and non-Roman Churches in India towards linking worship to the Indian situation.
    8.5. Principles for constructing experimental forms of worship.
9. Fasts and Feasts of the Church

    Advent, Christmas, Epiphany, Lent & Holy/Passion Week, Easter, Pentecost Sunday, Trinity and Trinity Sundays, Days of Saints, Harvest festival and other feasts.
10. Baptism

    Theological basis – historical practices – types of baptism – modes of baptism – the significance.
11. Lord's supper

    The institution of Lord's Supper - biblical basis - historical practices – when to take – how many times – the administration – the components – the steps to indigenize – the significance.

V. Core Textbooks

Forrest Beiser. *Worship of God.* New Delhi: Global University, 2005.

Joseph S. Carroll. *Christian Worship.* Bombay: Light of Life Books, 1989.

VI. Bibliography

Allen Ronald. *Worship - Rediscovering the Missing Jewel.* Oregon, Multnomah Press, 1979.

Allen, Ronald B. *The Wonder of Worship: A New Understanding of the Worship Experience.* Nashville, TN: Word Publishing, 2001.

Beiser, Forrest. *Worship of God.* Global University: New Delhi, 2004.

Best, Harold M. Unceasing Worship: Biblical Perspectives on Worship and the Arts. Downers Grove, IL: Intervarsity, 2003.

Bha, Bhakti Pancha Pushapanjali - 5 Orders of Worship. Madras, Gurukul Lutheran Theological, 1992.

Book of Common Worship. Louisville: Westminster/John Knox Press, 1993

Carroll, Joseph S. Christian Worship. Light of Life Books: Bombay, 1993.

Carson, D. A., ed. *Worship by the Book.* Grand Rapids, Michigan: Zondervan, 2002.

Carson, D.A., ed. *Worship: Adoration and Action.* Eugene, Oregon: Wipf & Stock, 2002.

Chamber Calvin H. *In Spirit and in Truth.* Ardmore: Dorrance and Company, 1980.

Davies J. G. *A New Dictionary of Liturgy and Worship:* London, SCM Press Ltd., 1986.

Dawn Marva J. Reaching Out without Dumbing Down - A Theology of Worship for this Urgent Time. USA, B. Eerdmans Publishing Co, 1995.

Deffener, Donald. *Sermons for Church Year Festivals:* USA: Concordia Publishing House, 1997.

Hurtado Larry W. *At The Origins of Christian Worship - The Context and Character of Earlier Christian Devotion.* Cumbria: Paternoster Publication, 1999.

Jones Bryn. *Worship- A Heart for God.* UK: Harvesttime, 1989.

Jones llion T. *A Historical Approach to Evangelical Worship.* New York: Abingdon Press, 1992.

Kauflin, Bob. *Worship Matters: Leading Others to Encounter the Greatness of God.* Wheaton, Illinois: Crossway Books, 2008.

Kendrick, Graham. *Learning to Worship - As a Way of Life.* Minnesota: Bethany Publish House, 1984.

Worship. England. Kings Way Publications Ltd, 1984.

Kidd, Reggie. *With One Voice: Discovering Christ's Song in Our Worship.* Grand Rapids, Michigan: Baker Books, 2005.

Liesch, Barry. *The New Worship: Straight Talk on Music and the Church.* Grand Rapids, Michigan: Baker Book House, 2001.

Lott, Eric J., *Worship in an Indian Context: Eight Inter-cultural Liturgies.* United Theological College, India, 1986.

Man, Ronald E. *Proclamation and Praise: Hebrews 2:12 and the Christology of Worship.* Eugene, Oregon: Wipf & Stock, 2002.

Murray, Paul Beasley. *Faith and Festivity- A guide for Today's Worship Leaders.* Eastbourme, Marc, 1991.

N. T. Wright, *For All God's Worth: True Worship and the Calling of the Church.* Eerdmans, 1997.

Osbeck, Kenneth W, *101 More Hymn Stories –The Inspiring Factual Backgrounds and Experiences that Prompted the Writing of 101 Favorite Hymns:* Secunderabad, OM Books, 1982.

Palmer W. *The Art of Conducting Public Worship.* New York: The Macmillan Company, 1993.

Perry, Michael. *Dramatised Bible Readings for Festivals.* n.p: Marshall Pickering, 1989.

Peterson, David. *Engaging With God: A Biblical Theology of Worship.* Downers Grove, IL: InterVarsity Press, 1992.

Piper, John. *Desiring God: Meditations of a Christian Hedonist.* Sisters, Oregon: Multnomah Books, 1986.

Smith, Delia. *A Feast For Lent – Bible Reading and Prayers for Every Day in Lent.* Oxford: Peter's way, 1983.

Underhill, Evelyn. *Worship*. Giildford: Eagle Publisher, 1991.

Webber, Robert E. *Worship Is A Verb: Eight Principles for Transforming Worship.* Peabody, Massachusetts: Hendrickson, 1992.

Webber, Robert. *Worship Old and New,* Zondervan, 1982.

White, James F. *Introduction to Christian Worship.* Nashville, TN: Abingdon Press, 1980.

Internal Assessments

Please read both the books and answer the following questions. Each question should be written in 1500 words and each carry 10% value.

1. Trace the development and changes in the Biblical forms of worship.
2. Write an essay about 'True Worship'.
3. If you are a pastor of a Church, how and what preparations will you make for a 'worship service'?

Attachment IV

Preaching of Sundar Singh
Lessons for Pastors and Preachers in a Nutshell

The Context of Sadhu Sundar Singh

a. The Missions and Missionaries
b. The British and Colonial Rule
c. The Native Religions and Cultures
d. The People and their Social Systems and Practices
e. The Regions and their Socio-Political and Economic Situation

Sundar Singh Life:

The Sadhu Image, decisive for him.

The Single Wandering Preacher, his personal choice.

The Devotional Life – would spend hours in silent meditation.

The Controversies – his sincerity was doubted by some in Europe.

The Form of Sundar Singh Preaching:

The Story Telling and Parables, innumerable stories, and anecdotes.

The Sharing of Personal Experience, his visions.

The Wonders and Miracles – always included.

The Content of Sundar Singh Preaching:

The Bible and Anecdotes

The Nature and Its Impact

The Visions of the Spiritual World

The Impact and Outcome

The Lessons

a. No Imitation
b. Deep Spirituality
c. Public Image
d. Signs of Times
e. Missionary Support/Church Support
f. Ecumenical Cooperation
g. Christ and Christ Alone
h. Total Commitment and Dedication
i. Not Counting the Cost
j. Faithful to the End

(Bishop P. Surya Prakash, a Bishop of the Church of South India, taught worship and preaching, New Testament and Speech Communication at the United Theological College in Bangalore between 1991 and 2000. His doctoral research in Germany was on the preaching of Sundar Singh.

The Preaching of Sadhu Sundar Singh: A Homiletic Analysis of Independent Preaching and Personal Christianity. Published by the Word Makers, Bengaluru 1991.

He is a leading authority on Sadhu Sundar Singh. He served as Bishop in Karimnagar of the Church of South India from 2007 to 2014. He lives with his wife in retirement in Hyderabad, Telangana State, India).

Some of the Books and Articles of the Author Published

The Preaching of Sadhu Sundar Singh, *A Homiletic Analysis of Independent Preaching and Personal Christianity*, Word Makers, Bangalore 1991 (A Doctoral Dissertation done in Germany).

Sermon Preparation: Biblical Preaching, Methodological Issues and Perspectives, in, The South India Churchman, August 1991, pp. 6-9; and in Bangalore Theological Forum, Bangalore. Vol. xxiii, No. 3, Sept. 1991, pp. 25-37.

Preaching in India - Problems and Perspectives, in, Masihi Sevak, Pastoral Journal United Theological College, vol. XVI No.1 March 1992, pp. 1–11.

Church of South India, *Synod Worship Order Books*, 1992, 1994, and 1996. CSI Synod Publications, held in Palayam Kottai, Tiruchirapalli and Coimbatore respectively.

Sermon Accountability: Responsibility of the Congregation towards its Ministry of Preaching, Bangalore Theological Forum, vol. 24, issues 3 and 4, 1992, pp. 62-74; National Council of Churches Review vol. Cxiii No.1, 1993, pp. 36-53; Kristu Jyothi, A Youth Pastoral Theological Catechetical Journal, vol. 8, No. 3, 1992, pp. 35-51.

Implications of Revival Preaching in India, South India Churchman, June-July 1993, pp. 3-6, NCC Review Vol. CXV, No. 3, March 1994, pp. 180-190; 205-207.

Homiletics and Preaching in India, in, Concise Encyclopaedia of Preaching, editors William H. Willimon and Richard Lischer, Westminster and Knox Press 1995, pp. 238-241.

Be an Active Church Member, in, South India Churchman, CSI Synod, June-July 1996, pp. 13-15.

Preaching from the Lectionary, in, South India Churchman, CSI Synod, August-September 1996, pp. 15-19.

Bible Studies on Spiritual Renewal Notes, in, South India Churchman, CSI Synod, October 1996 pp. 11-12

Ongoing Ministerial Formation, in, South India Churchman, CSI Synod, November 1996, pp. 11-13

Expository Preaching in Indian Context, in, South India Churchman, CSI Synod, December 1996, pp. 9-11.

Gospel Sharing in Pluralist Society Today - Toward a New Homiletic, in, Greater Peace, Closer Fellowship and Fuller Life, editors Lily and Sam Amirtham, CSI Golden Jubilee Publication, 1997, pp. 188-198.

Unite-Liberate-Celebrate, A Guide for the Study of the Golden Jubilee Theme, CSI Synod 1997, edited by P. Surya Prakash. CSI Synod Publications.

Liturgy and Worship of the Church of South India, in, United to Unite, History of the Church of South India 1947-1997, pp.127-132, edited by J. W. Gladstone.

Renewal and Reformation of Liturgies in the Historical and Pluralistic Context, in, Liturgical Renewal in the Indian Church, a special issue of Masihi Sevak, UTC Bengaluru, edited by Samson Prabhakar, December 1998, pp. 19-31; The South India Churchman, April 1997, pp. 7-10.

Questions on Sermon Analysis – A Viable Form of Sermon Development, in, Masihi Sevak, UTC Bangalore 1999, vol. xxiv, No. 2, pp. 65-70.

New Trends in Christian Ministry: Homiletics and Preaching, in, Challenges and Responses, Churches Ministry in the Third Millennium: Implications for Theological Education, editor Gnana Robinson, UTC Bangalore, Jubilee Volume, 2000, pp. 587-612.

Towards Understanding "Ecumenism" as Mission of the Church, in, Ecumenism: Prospects and Challenges, ISPCK 2001, edited by Vinod Victor et.al. pp. xv-xxiii.

Ecumenism: Prospects and Challenges, ISPCK 2001, edited by Vinod Victor, Leslie Nathaniel, and P. Surya Prakash, published by the CSI Synod, ISPCK 2001.

Sadhu Sundar Singh's Contribution, in, Christianity is Indian. The Emergence of an Indigenous Community, edited by Roger E. Hedlund, Revised edition, ISPCK 2004 pp. 113-128.

Fullness of Life, CSI Synod, 2004, sermons and Bible Studies preached at the CSI Synod meetings Bangalore 2004, edited by Mathew Varkey, CSI Synod Publication.

The Episcopacy in the Church of South India: A Reflection by a CSI Presbyter: My Vision of Episcopacy in the CSI, in, Shepherd of a Pilgrim People, Essays in Honour of Bishop J.W.Gladstone, editors Gideon Shobhanam and Vinod Victor, published by ISPCK, for CSI South Kerala Diocese 2005, pp. 55-70.

Church in India: Is it a Visible Sign of the Invisible Grace of God? in, The God of All Grace, Essays in honour of Origen Vasantha Jathanna, edited by Joseph George, Asian Trading Corporation, Bengaluru 2005, pp. 475-488.

Spirit of Lent, in, Mount of Olives, our Lenten journey with Jesus, ICSA Books, Chennai 2009, pp. 1-4.

Church of South India, One Church, One Faith, One Lord, in, CSI Life, Magazine of the Church of South India, September 2011, pp. 2-7

Where is Ecumenism Heading in India, Christian Folk, vol. 22, issue no.1st January 2020, pp. 4-7.

The Office of a Bishop in Church of South India: A Personal Reflection by a Bishop, The Pilgrim, May & October 2021, pp. 84-100.

Insights for Observing the time of Lent in Christian Tradition, Pilgrim Magazine, published by the Friends of the Church in India, London, April 2022.

Attachment V

Theses Written in India on Preaching and are Available in Archives of the United Theological College, Bengaluru, Karnataka State, India (by Courtesy of Mr. Prabhu, Librarian UTC Bengaluru).

Zuankamang, Daimai. Analysis of Preaching in Selected Churches of Liangmai in.. Thesis. West Bengal: Senate of Serampore College, 2007. (251, ZUA / M.TH.).

Bagh, Premanand. Analysis of Present-Day Preaching in the Bharatiya General Conference Mennonite Church in Madhya Pradesh With... to Church's Teaching on 'Peace'. Serampore: Senate of Serampore College, 1992. (251, BAG/MTH).

John, Varughese. Analysis of the Sermons of St. John Chrysostom on Social Issues and Their Relevance for Preaching Today [THESIS]. Serampore: Senate of Serampore College, 1993 (252, JOH/MTH).

Stephen, A Alfred. Appraisal of Liberation Preaching of Bishop Desmond Tutu and Rev. Allan Boesak [THESIS]. Serampore: Senate of Serampore College, 1994 (252, STE/MTH).

Thanchhungi, S. Appraisal of the Preaching Ministry of the Mizo Select Evangelistic Groups in Mizoram [THESIS]. Serampore: Senate of Serampore College, 1996. (251, THA/MTH).

Bhimappa, Devaputhra. Assessment of Contemporary Christian Preaching in Selected Churches in Bangalore [THESIS]. Serampore: Senate of Serampore College, 1997 (251, BHI/MTH).

Vijayakumar, Christian Crispus. Assessment of Contemporary Preaching in Christian and .... Thesis. West Bengal: Senate of Seramore, 2008 (252, VIJ / M.TH.).

Karunashri, S K. Assessment of Lay Involvement in the Ministry of Preaching in Selected Congregations of Mennonite Brethren Church in AP [THESIS]. Serampore: Senate of Serampore College, 1994 (262.15, KAR/MTH).

Iswari, Nirala. Assessment of Preaching of HAPHRAM/ KOTHABAIGRA and SUKUBAR GERJA DOIDENGRA/ HAPHRAM HINJAO Among Bodos in Northern Evangelical Lutheran Church [THESIS. Serampore: Senate of Serampore College, 1997 (251, ISW/MTH).

John, E. C. Christian Hope and Its Relevance to Christian Preaching Today [THESIS]. Serampore: Np, 1954 (236, JOH/ BD).

Devakumar, Stanley J. Communication Methods Used By the Tamil Evangelical Lutheran Churches (T.E.L.C) With Special Reference to Preaching (Thesis). Wet Bengal: Senate of Seramore, 2011 (254.3, DEV / M.TH.).

Butesen, Communication Skills in Preaching with Reference to Churches in Mokokchung [THESIS]. Bangalore: United Theological College, 2008 (254.3, BUT/BD).

Mohan, A. Communication Strategies for the Ministry of Preaching with Special Reference to the Evangelical Church of India in Madras Today. West Bengal: Senate of Serampore College, 1997 (254.3, MOH / M.TH.).

Alberts, Ivan P. J. Counselling Through Preaching: A Study of Selected Preachers in and Around Bangalore [THESIS]. Serampore: Senate of Serampore College, 1992 (253.5, ALB/ MTH).

Vanlalzauva, Th. Effects of Preaching in the Life of Lai Christian Community: An Appraisal [THESIS]. Serampore: Senate of Serampore College, 1998 (251, VAN/MTH).

Ravi Kumar, Daniel S. Homiletical Analysis of Preaching in Movement Towards the Formation of the Church of South India 1910-1947 [THESIS]. Serampore: Senate of Serampore College, 1996 (251, RAV/MTH).

Bangera, Abraham Vinayalal. Laity Response to Pastoral Preaching in the United Basel Mission Church of South Kanara and Coorg [THESIS]. Serampore: Senate of Serampore College, 1998 (251, BAN/MTH).

Varghese, Saju. Narrative Preaching and Its Relevance in Selected Churches. Thesis. West Bengal: Senate of Seramore, 2009 (275.4, VAR / M.TH.).

Wungnaowung, A. S. Pastoral Preaching in the Tangkhul Naga Baptist Churches. Thesis. West Bengal: Senate of Serampore College, 2008 (253.5, WUN / M.TH.).

Kuriakose, K. J. Patterns of Preaching in the Indian Pentecostal Church of God in Kerala [THESIS]. Serampore: Senate of Serampore College, 2000. (251, KUR/MTH).

Bright, B M. Preaching Ministry of Jesus in the Gospel (mathew 5:13-16) and Its Implications for Pastoral Ministry in the CSI South Kerala Diocese (thesis). Bangalore: United Theological College, 2018 (226.2, BRI/BD).

Philip, V. P. Preaching as Communication: Youth Perspectives on Preaching in Select Pentecostal Churches in Kerala [THESIS]. Serampore: Senate of Serampore College, 2007 (254.3, PHI/ MTH).

Noklenyongdang, Preaching of Rev. Longri Ao: Analysis and Its Relevance to Naga Baptist Churches Today [THESIS]. Serampore: Senate of Serampore College, 2000 (252, NOK/MTH).

Surya Prakash, Perumalla. Preaching of Sadhu Sundar Singh: A Homiletic Analysis of Independent Preaching and Personal Christianity [THESIS]. Bielefeld: Kirchliche Hochschule Bethel, 1990 (251, SUR/DTH).

Surya Prakash, Perumalla. Relationship Between Pastoral Counselling and Preaching [THESIS]. Serampore: Np, 1976 (253.5, SUR/BD).

Samuel, N A. Resurrection of the Body and Its Significance in the Preaching of the Gospel in India [THESIS]. Serampore: Np, 1953 (251, SAM/BD).

Darngawn, Lalchawimawia. Revival Preaching By El-Bethel Team in Chanmari and Dawrpui.Thesis. West Bengal: Senate of Serampore College, 2007 (275.416, DAR / M.TH.).

Zalawma, H. Role of Doctrinal Preaching in the Mizoram Presbyterian Church to Counter Sectarianism [THESIS]. Serampore: Senate of Serampore College, 1992 (230.5, ZAL/ MTH).

Sangma, Dilseng M. Role of Preaching for the Holistic Growth of the Church with ... Thesis. West Bengal: Senate of Seramore, 2010 (305.8009, SAN / M.TH.).

Mingthing, Y. L. Role of Preaching in the Development of the Church Among the Tangkhul Nagas of Manipur [THESIS]. Serampore: Np, 1977 (251, MIN/MTH).

Zorammawia, C. Role of Singing in the Preaching Ministry of Mizoram Presbyterian Church [THESIS]. Serampore: Senate of Serampore College, 2000 (251, ZOR/MTH).

Luke, Manoranjan. Study of Lay Expectation Factors in Relation to Preaching in Bangalore and Suggestions for the Ministry of Preaching [THESIS]. Serampore: Np, 1981 (250, LUK/MTH).

Daniel, C. Study of the Interpretation of Karma in Modern Buddhism in Relation to the Preaching of the Christian Doctrine of Atonement to Buddhists [THESIS]. Serampore: Np, 1956 (291.22, DAN/BD).

Amirtham, S. Value of the Category of Sacrifice in Christian Preaching in India [THESIS]. Serampore: Np, 1956 (251, AMI/ BD).

Hyderabad
May 2025

Biography

The Rt. Rev. Dr. P. Surya Prakash

Church Affiliation: Church of South India, Medak Diocese.

1. Education

a. Primary School

First teacher at Christunagar was Sri Mamilla Shanthiah Panthulu.

Primary School 1958-61 at CSI High School, Nizamabad:

b. Higher Secondary School

Multipurpose (Pre-University Certificate), Wesley Boy's High School, Secunderabad.

c. University

i. B.A. (English Literature as major) Nizam's College, Osmania University, Hyderabad.

   C.C. (Certificate in Counselling) Christian Counselling Centre Vellore, Tamil Nadu in 1975.

   Theological Education and Ministerial Formation:

ii. B.D. Diploma United Theological College, Bangalore, Karnataka (1972-76) with first class in 1976.

B.D. Degree Serampore College, Serampore, West Bengal with higher second class in 1976.

C. P. E. Boston Cluster for Clinical Pastoral Education at the Boston University School of Theology, Boston, U.S.A. in 1982.

M.Th. Post-graduate Diploma United Theological College, Bangalore with higher second class in 1983 with scholarship from the Senate of Serampore College (1981-82).

iii. M.Th. Degree Serampore College, Serampore, West Bengal and Boston University School of Theology, US.A. with specialization in the New Testament, with higher second class in 1984 with scholarship from Global Ministries of the Methodist Church USA and Boston University.

P. N. D. S. Prüfung zum Nachweis deutscher Sprachkenntnisse, Studienkolleg des ökumenischen Studienwerks, Bochum, Federal Republic of Germany, certificate for admission to the German Universities in 1987.

Being sent by the Diocese and having been sponsored by the United Theological College Bangalore under the leadership of then Principal Dr. E. C. John, completed (1987-90),

iv. Dr. of Theology. Kirchliche Hochschule Bethel, Bielefeld Germany with specialization in Homiletics (Preaching) with Cum Laude in December 1990.

d. Other Training Programmes and Apprenticeships

Rural Evangelism, Ambur, Tamil Nadu, in April 1973.

Industrial Relations, Gurukul Lutheran Theological College, Madras, Tamil Nadu, in April 1974.

Suicide Prevention Course and Praxis, St. Martha's Hospital Bangalore, January – April 1974.

Hospital Chaplaincy, Christian Medical College Hospital, Vellore, January – February 1975.

Workshop on Communication, Medak, in January 1978.

Workshop on Preaching, Gurukul Theological College and Research Institute, Madras (Chennai), January 1979 led by Dr. Peter Moritzon, Germany.

Holy Land Study Seminar in Israel, April – May 1984 led by Dr. T. N. Swanson. This visit to Holy Land made profound impact on my ministry.

Various Seminars and Workshops of the Ecumenical Scholarship Foundation Bochum, in Germany, Switzerland and Belgium from 1986 to 1990 (see Appendix below).

Staff Institute on Communication of the Board of Theological Education of the Senate of Serampore College, Bangalore, April – May 1992 led by Dr. C. R. W. David, Prof. Keval Kumar and others.

Speech Communication, Princeton Theological Seminary, Princeton, New Jersey, U.S.A., April – June 1993 guided by Prof. Dr. Charles Bartow.

2. Pastoral Ministry and Professional Experience

a. Ministerial Candidate in 1972

b. Village Experience during Theological Training

May 1973 in Shakkarnagar Pastorate under the guidance of Rev. A. C. Dayanand, the presbyter in charge.

May 1974 in Kamareddy Pastorate under the guidance of Rev. M. Anandam, the presbyter in charge.

May 1974 in Dudgaon Pastorate under the guidance of Rev. N. S. Mathew the presbyter in charge and Rev. K. James Christopher, Presbyter in Sonnapet.

c. Ordination

August 18, 1976, ordained as deacon of the Church of South India at the CSI Wesley Church, Secunderabad, by the Moderator of the CSI the Most Rev. Ananda Rao Samuel, organised by the Rev. G. B. Devasahayam, the Moderator's Commissory of the Diocese.

1976 – 1977 Deacon, Church of South India Medak Diocese, Varni; Shakkarnagar Pastorate – rural context, under the guidance of Rev. M. P. Srinivasa Rao, Presbyter in charge.

July 31, 1977, ordained as Presbyter of the Church of South India at CSI Church Dudgaon by the Rt. Rev. B. G. Prasada Rao, Bishop in Medak. The sermon was preached by the Rev. B. P. Sugandhar, now Bishop in Medak and Moderator of the CSI.

1977 – 1980 Presbyter, Church of South India Medak Diocese, Adilabad under the guidance of Rev. K.J. Joseph, Presbyter in charge.

Adilabad Pastorate – rural and urban context. During this period, the congregation became an independent pastorate in Godavary DCC.

Having been sent by the Diocese was from January 1991 to 2000 – theological educator at the United Theological College, Bangalore.

d. Probation 1976 – 80

Trial Sermons and worship services:

1976 at CSI Church in Nizamabad, Supervisor Rev. D. I. Swamidass.

1977 at CSI Church in Luxettipett, Supervisor Rev. T. B. Prabhakar Rao.

1978 at CSI Church in Nirmal, Supervisor Rev. M. P. Sanjeeva Rao.

1979 at CSI Church in Luxettipett, Supervisor Rev. M. P. Srinivasa Rao.

1981 – 1982 Student Pastor, United Methodist Church of All Nations, Boston, U.S.A. – urban context.

1982 – 1986 Presbyter, Church of South India Medak Diocese, Bellampalli; Bellampalli Pastorate – semi-urban and industrial context, under the guidance of Rev. D. I. Prabhudass Presbyter in charge between 1982-84.

Became Presbyter in Charge in 1984 for Bellampalli and Mandamarri pastorates (1984-86).

1986 – 1990 Guest Preacher at different congregations in Germany. Participant and resource person at several national and international seminars.

1991 – 1993 Associate Presbyter, Church of South India Karnataka Central Diocese, St. Peter's Telugu Church, Bangalore. Regular preacher at this church till 2000.

1991 – 1999 Regular preacher at St. Mark's Cathedral Bangalore; churches and conferences in India.

1992 – 1996 Resource person to the Pastoral Aid Programme of the Methodist Church in India. Worked closely with the then Director the Rt. Rev. S. V. Sampath Kumar, Bishop in Bangalore.

1992 – 1999 Resource person and consultant to the Pastoral Aid Department of the Church of South India which organises the continuing education programme and pastoral study and reflection of the pastors.

1993 April – July: Guest Preacher at different congregations in New Jersey, Washington, D. C., Chicago, Denver, Loveland and San Francisco in U.S.A.; and Germany.

1997 June – July: Guest Preacher at different congregations in San Francisco Bay Area in U.S.A.

1997 October – February 1998: Guest Preacher at different congregations and resource person at meetings and consultations/ seminars of Evangelische Lutherische Mission in Hermannsburg; ökumenisches Studienwerk in Bochum; Missions akademie in Hamburg; and Kirchliche Hochschule Bethel, Germany, during the sabbatical year.

May 2000 - Regular Preacher at different congregations and resource person at meetings and consultations/seminars in Germany on Theology, Missiology, Dalit Theology, Inter-religious Dialogue and Relations, Partnership Relations, Ecumenical relationships, Third World Theology, Economy, Political and cultural life etc.

2000 – 2005 Chaplain and Officiating Minister at St. Catherines English Church Stuttgart with permission and authorisation by the Bishop Jeffrey, Diocese of Europe of the Anglican Church.

2000 – 2005 Member of the Council of the Anglican and Episcopal Churches in Europe.

3. Teaching Ministry

a. Theological Educator

1991–1992 Lecturer in New Testament and Christian Ministry at UTC.

1991–1999 Resource person at the Indian School of Ecumenical Theology of the Ecumenical Christian Centre, Whitefield, Bangalore.

1992–1997 Associate Professor of Homiletics at the United Theological College, Bangalore, India; teaching subjects like New Testament, Liturgy and Worship, Christian Education, Homiletics and Preaching; Pastoral Administration; Speech Communication etc. at the Graduate and the Post-graduate levels, i.e., Bachelor of divinity and master's in theology.

1997–1999 Professor of Homiletics/Preaching at UTC:

During 1990 – 2000, Trained nearly 250 students at B.D. level and 25 students in homiletics and preaching at M.Th. level at UTC.

1996 – 1999 Visiting Faculty/course writer/consultant at the St. Andrew Centre for Human Resource Development and Counselling of the India Sunday School Union, Coonoor, a national organisation for Christian Education in India.

1996 – 1999 Course writer and resource person at the post-graduate level programme of the Association of Theological Education by Extension (TAFTEE), Bangalore.

1996 – 1999 Resource person at the South Asia Theological and Research Institute (SATHRI) Bangalore; the doctoral programme of the Board of Theological Education of the Senate of Serampore.

1997 June – July: Visiting professor at San Francisco Theological Seminary, U.S.A.; taught a course on "Christian Preaching in a Pluralist context" to the D.Min. candidates.

1997 October – February 1998: Visiting professor at Missions seminar Hermannsburg and Kirchliche Hochschule Bethel in Germany; taught courses in German on Asian Christian Preachers; Asian Spirituality and Homiletics.

1998 - 2000 Resource person and visiting faculty for the D.Min. Programme of the Senate of Serampore.

Principles of Preaching Today

Better Preaching, Better Worship

Better Preaching, Better Church

Better Preaching, Better Theology

Better Preaching, Better Witness

Better Preaching, Better Involvement

Better Preaching, Better Administration

Better Preaching, Better Mission

Better Preaching, Better Life

Better Preaching, Better Communion

Better Preaching, Better Church, and Society

Preacher's Commitment and Dedication

"Do your best to present yourself to God as one approved, a worker who has no need to be ashamed, rightly handling the word of truth."
2 Timothy 2.15

"For since, in the wisdom of God, the world did not know God through wisdom, it pleased God through the folly of what we preach to save those who believe."
1 Corinthians 1.21

"And I, when I came to you, brothers, did not come proclaiming to you the testimony of God with lofty speech or wisdom. For I decided to know nothing among you except Jesus Christ and him crucified. And I was with you in weakness and in fear and much trembling, and my speech and my message were not in plausible words of wisdom, but in demonstration of the Spirit and of power, so that your faith might not rest in the wisdom of men but in the power of God. ..."
1 Corinthians 2.1-8

"And I, when I came to you, brothers, did not come proclaiming to you the testimony of God with lofty speech or wisdom. For I decided to know nothing among you except Jesus Christ and him crucified. And I was with you in weakness and in fear and much trembling, and my speech and my message were not in plausible words of wisdom, but in demonstration of the Spirit and of power,

so that your faith might not rest in the wisdom of men but in the power of God. ..."
Romans 1.16

"But we preach Christ crucified, a stumbling block to Jews and folly to Gentiles,"
1 Corinthians 1.23

"Some indeed preach Christ from envy and rivalry, but others from good will. The latter do it out of love, knowing that I am put here for the defense of the gospel. The former proclaim Christ out of selfish ambition, not sincerely but thinking to afflict me in my imprisonment. What then? Only that in every way, whether in pretense or in truth, Christ is proclaimed, and in that I rejoice. Yes, and I will rejoice,"
Philippians 1.15-18.

(All verses are from the English Standard Version of the Bible).